ACTING
SOLO

HAL HOLBROOK

as

"MARK TWAIN TONIGHT!"

A Re-creation of America's Greatest Humorist

PAT CARROLL

in

GERTRUDE STEIN
GERTRUDE STEIN
GERTRUDE STEIN

by

Marty Martin

John Gielgud

Shakespeare's
"ages of man"

LILY TOMLIN
In
The Search for Signs of
Intelligent Life In The Universe
Written by
JANE WAGNER

ACTING SOLO

THE ART OF ONE-MAN SHOWS

BY JORDAN R. YOUNG

INTRODUCTION BY JULIE HARRIS

MOONSTONE PRESS

ACTING SOLO
The Art of One-Man Shows

FIRST EDITION

Published by Moonstone Press
P.O. Box 142, Beverly Hills CA 90213

Copyright © 1989 by Jordan R. Young

Introduction copyright © 1989 by Julie Harris

Portions of the chapter Homage to Beckett are excerpted from *The Beckett Actor*, copyright © 1987 by Jordan R. Young.

Cover photograph by Sy Friedman
Julie Harris as Emily Dickinson in *The Belle of Amherst*,
spreading hands "to gather paradise."

Designed by Jack Ritchard
Typeset by Suzette Mahr, Words & Deeds, Los Angeles, California

Manufactured in the United States of America

PN
1936
Y68
1989

Library of Congress Cataloging-in-Publication Data
Young, Jordan R.
    Acting Solo : the art of one-man shows / by Jordan R. Young : introduction by Julie Harris. — 1st ed.
    p.   cm.
    Bibliography: p.
    Includes index.
    ISBN 0-940410-84-2 (alk. paper) : $21.95 — ISBN 0-940410-85-0 (pbk. : alk. paper) : $11.95
    1. Monodramas—History and criticism. 2. Acting. I. Title.
PN1936.Y68 1989
792'.028—dc20   89-8363
                                                          CIP

The paper used in this publication meets the minimum requirements of American National Standards for Information Sciences, Permanance of Paper for Printed Library Materials ANSI Z39.48-1984

10 9 8 7 6 5 4 3 2 1

Introduction

It's March 1989, and I am on tour in San Francisco with *Driving Miss Daisy* and there are three actors in the play — and now I'm trying to remember the first time I saw a solo performance. I think it must have been the great Ruth Draper, who wrote her own material and performed the monologues across America in the thirties and forties to the delight of her audiences. Miss Draper was extraordinary. Now Lily Tomlin and Whoopi Goldberg are keeping that tradition alive — telling stories about ladies different from Miss Draper's ladies of society. Lily and Whoopi have gone into the city streets, and they people the stage with the aristocrats of hard times and amuse and move us with their marvelous, creative power. We see many characters on the stage and yet there is only one person there in front of us for the evening.

I've been swept away by Emlyn Williams' Charles Dickens, Hal Holbrook's Mark Twain, Roy Dotrice's *Brief Lives* and most recently, Spalding Gray's *Swimming to Cambodia*.

Acting solo is really the art of storytelling. When I was first introduced to the solo play I was fortunate to work with a great and inspired director, Charles Nelson Reilly, who made the process of rehearsing such a play a voyage of discovery and a joy. I was already in love with the material, the poems and the letters of Emily Dickinson — and that is the magic ingredient for me — to be *in love* with your subject. I have played — solo — not only Emily Dickinson but Charlotte Brontë, both in plays by William Luce, and Sonia Tolstoy — wife of Count Leo Tolstoy, the great Russian novelist — in *The Countess* by Donald Freed. All three ladies — Emily, Charlotte, Sonia — I love intensely. I wouldn't want to do a solo play about a lady with whom I wasn't totally in love.

The first time I found myself *alone* on stage was when I performed *The Belle of Amherst*. We opened the tour in Seattle, Washington, at the Moore Egyptian Theatre, February 1976. As I came on stage, with my tea tray, in a rush of energy and faced the audience, I was overwhelmed and even lost my place in the script — but almost immediately found my strength and then it became fun for me. It was like visiting a good friend and I was always thrilled to be part of Miss Dickinson's world. Toward the last part of the play — where the poetry and language becomes so luminous — I always felt I was riding a magic carpet, floating through the air, and the journey would have no end.

Acting solo is a compelling way of telling a story, intensely personal, and one that conveys itself vividly to an audience. I am sure we will always be surprised by the artists who come along, who will amuse and thrill us by this form of theatre.

Julie Harris

Contents

Introduction by Julie Harris   5

Preface   9

Prologue   13

The Art of Acting Solo   21

The Queen and her Disciples   37

In Person   51

Will the Real Mark Twain Please Stand Up?   69

Homage to the Bard   83

Monologue: Pat Carroll   99

The Irish Tradition   115

Emily, Charlotte, Zelda and Lillian   129

Homage to Beckett   147

Monologue: Ray Stricklyn   151

Life as Art   173

Epilogue   189

Appendix   195

Bibliography   201

Index   207

About the Author

Jordan R. Young is a prolific freelance writer whose work has appeared in The Los Angeles Times, The New York Times, The Washington Post, The Christian Science Monitor and dozens of other publications. He is the author of several books on the performing arts, including *Spike Jones and his City Slickers, Reel Characters, Let Me Entertain You* and *The Beckett Actor*. He is co-author of the new one-woman play, *Twilight at Steepletop: The Passions of Edna St. Vincent Millay*.

Preface

My wife seldom has to be persuaded to spend an evening at the theatre, but she practically had to be dragged to *An Evening with Quentin Crisp*. "A man standing on stage talking about himself? That's what we're going to see?" I had no idea what we were going to see — or hear. I only knew that it was not to be missed, having seen *The Naked Civil Servant*, the TV film of Crisp's outrageous autobiography.

The Solari Theatre in Beverly Hills played host to the typical opening night crowd that evening — blue jeans and mink stoles. They had no more expectation than I did, and they were not disappointed. "Television is a redemptive medium," Crisp told the audience. "It sanctifies anyone who appears on it. So if you have a habit of which you are terribly ashamed, don't do it in secret. Do it on television..."

Following the intermission he fielded queries from the audience, as deftly as a ballplayer catching long fly balls. At the end of the evening, he agreed to take one last question. Actor Red Buttons jumped from his front row seat and shouted, "Would you please repeat the last two hours?" Even my wife approved the request.

That a non-actor like Quentin Crisp could hold the stage with such presence was a revelation. On another occasion, Rudy Vallee proved to us that a man standing on the stage talking about himself could be a awful bore. How well I remember those two solo programs — two unforgettable evenings in the theatre, at opposite ends of the spectrum.

The idea for *Acting Solo* grew out of a project which altered my perspective on theatre and one-person shows — a play with a cast of one, which I was asked to help create. The Epilogue to this book is a brief first-person account of the creation process — which threatened the sanity of the author when the play went into rehearsals during the writing of the book.

The deeper involved in the development of the play I became, the more I thought about the dozens of solo shows I had seen over the years and began to ponder different aspects of them. I did not write this book because I had something I wanted to say about this form of theatre, nor did I know what shape the book would ultimately take. I wrote it because I did not know. It was an expedition into largely uncharted territory that provoked my curiosity more with each step into the dark.

Special thanks are due Julie Harris, for graciously taking time from her demanding schedule to write the introduction for this book; Pat Carroll, for being her delightful self, an interviewer's dream; William Luce, for discussing his work at length, and for his constant thoughtfulness and support; and Mark W. Travis, for his generosity in expanding my definition of theatre.

I am grateful to those who contributed interviews: Scott Alsop, Fred Curchack, John Gielgud, Spalding Gray, Paul Linke, Shane McCabe, Barry McGovern, Gloria MacGowran, Jack MacGowran, Bill McLinn, Eamon Morrissey, Ray Reinhardt, George Spota and Ray Stricklyn.

Thanks are due also to the following individuals and organizations: Bettye Ackerman, Janie Apodaca, Janice Arkatov, Sherrye Cimino, Jim Curtis, David Drummond, Shay Duffin, Jim Fox, Ian Frost, Michael Gostlin, Peter Hagen, Hal Holbrook, Garrett Lee, Donald McWhinnie, Wolf Mankowitz, Jude Narita, Carroll O'Connor, Ted Post, Ellen Ratner, Mort Rosenthal, Rebecca Schull, Bill Shick, Randy Skretvedt, Benjamin Stewart, Bill Studdiford, Philip Young, Barry Yourgrau; Margaret Herrick Library, Academy of Motion Picture Arts and Sciences; American Theatre Press; Bonfils Theatre; British Broadcasting Company; Caroline Cornish, BBC Written Archives; British Library; Capital Cities/ABC; Chapman College; Cherry Lane Theatre; Cinecom Pictures; Cleveland Press; Consolidated Poster; Bruce Campbell, Merle Debuskey & Associates; Joan Simmons, EIS Presentations; Larry Edmunds Bookshop; Folger Shakespeare Library; Charles Kuhnel, Front Row Center; Lauren Mueller, Goodman Theatre; Grove Theatre Company; Los Angeles Theatre Center; Mark Taper Forum; Metro-Goldwyn-Mayer; Klaus W. Kolmar, Namco Booking; New York Public Library at Lincoln Center; Joyce H. Crawford, Odyssey Theatre Ensemble; Performing Arts; Playbill; Solari Theatre Ensemble; Universal Pictures.

Finally, I am indebted to my wife, Pam, who deserves an award for putting up with me during the writing of this book.

Jordan R. Young
Los Angeles
1989

Prologue

The one-man show might well appear to be an American invention — some would say a conceit — of the twentieth century, whereby an actor may showcase his talents and insure himself of an income. Yet this unique form of theatre originated and flourished in England over 200 years ago.

Few opportunities existed for the eighteenth century English actor who was not attached to one of two London theatres licensed by the king; the Theatre Royal (later the Drury Lane) and the rival Lincoln's Inn Fields Theatre held by patent the sole right to perform legitimate drama, since the Restoration. The first one-man "entertainments" were devised as means of circumventing these restrictions.

British satirist Samuel Foote (1721-1777) has been credited as the originator of the vogue. A contemporary of famed actor-manager David Garrick, Foote was a failed tragedian, a short, round man whose acting debut as Othello provoked laughter. He found his métier in *The Rehearsal*, a burlesque in which he mimicked several well-known actors — as was customary in the role — as well as statesmen and other public figures.

This success prompted Foote to present *The Diversions of the Morning*, a satirical revue consisting of his take-offs, at the unlicensed Theatre in the Hay-Market on April 22, 1747. When the patent theatres threatened to interfere, he staged matinees which would not compete with their evening performances; he further evaded the Licensing Act by inviting friends to "come and drink a dish of chocolate" with him, and then proceeded to do his imitations under the pretense of "training some young performers for the stage."

Foote's shows were not strictly solo — he was joined by a small company — but they were built around his talent for mimicry. For the next 30 years Foote wrote and performed a series of vicious and highly successful entertainments, in which he ridiculed artists, preachers, physicians, noblemen and socialites. Garrick was a favorite target. Try as they might, Foote's victims were unable to put a stop to his unflattering lampoons; when a noted printer and publisher took legal action after being caricatured as Peter Paragraph, the actor made a mockery of the trial proceedings on stage.

Foote was not the only one to overstep the licensing laws of the period. He inspired a rash of imitators, including mimic Tate Wilkinson, who played small parts with Garrick and toured with Foote before he became famous in his own right; George Saville Carey, who impersonated actors and vocalists in his *Lecture on Mimicry*; and Harry Woodward, a comedian who wrote harlequinades for Garrick before soloing in burlesques and topical skits.

It was George Alexander Stevens (1710-1784), however, who first popularized the monologuist's art with his celebrated *Lecture upon Heads* — which promptly became an unauthorized staple of solo entertainers throughout the English-speaking world.

Stevens, a mediocre actor by all accounts, performed with provincial troupes and acted in Garrick's company before catapulting himself to fame and fortune. He also

G.A. Stevens' *Lecture upon Heads*, as performed circa 1765.

wrote plays for puppet theatre — which enjoyed great popularity in eighteenth century England — and novels like *The Adventures of a Speculist*, which satirized the follies of the age and London character types.

Calling upon a succession of papier-mâché heads, wig blocks and hand props, Stevens first presented his *Lecture* on April 30, 1764 at the Little Theatre in the Hay-Market. It was designed with sophisticated audiences in mind, filled with classical and literary references, puns, word play and comic jargon.

In the course of his two-hour monologue Stevens poked fun at famous people (Alexander the Great) and social stereotypes (an Indian chief, a lawyer, a conjurer, a fishwife); exhibited the quack doctor's coat of arms — three ducks; launched into a discourse on nothing, "which the exhibiter hopes he has properly executed, by making nothing of it"; discussed women's hats; gave a dissertation on sneezing and snuff-taking; and harangued the audience in a vicious impersonation of a methodist parson.

Stevens' *Lecture upon Heads* "was an instantaneous and resounding success, to be quoted, pirated, adapted, printed, revised, spun-off and satirized for the next half century," according to scholar Gerald Kahan, who has calculated that the program received, in whole or part, nearly 1,000 performances.

Owing to the absence of copyright laws, male and female imitators — and even child entertainers — presented variations on G.A. Stevens' one-man show throughout England, Ireland, India, Canada and America (where it was first performed in 1766). Many actors down on their luck used the comic farrago to keep their creditors at bay; some claimed to be Stevens, while others asserted he was a partner in their profits or that he had sold the rights to them.

James Solas Dodd delivered *A Satyrical Lecture on Hearts* (to which he later appended *A Critical Dissertation on Noses*) while John Palmer toured with a version entitled *Portraits of the Living and Dead*. John Collins modeled his cabaret-style evening of songs, monologues and imitations after Stevens, presenting it variously as *The Evening Brush* and *Lecture upon Oratory*. Other performers delivered *A Lecture on Tails* and *A Lecture upon No-Heads*.

Charles Dibdin (1745-1814) staged puppet shows, like

Stevens, prior to devising his one-man *Readings and Music* (1787), with which he toured the English provinces. He soon built his own theatre in London, the Sans Souci, where he continued to perform solo. His shows — which consisted of monologues, impersonations, anecdotes and songs, with Dibdin accompanying himself at the piano and harpsicord — were presented in the manner of private drawing-room entertainment; following a precedent set by Samuel Foote, many of the programs were based on his tours.

In the early nineteenth century, Charles Mathews (1776-1835) established himself as *the* comedian of the age with an original form of entertainment, once described as "a whole play in the person of one man." He was a unique entity: Samuel Taylor Coleridge called him "a comic poet, acting his own poems."

A born mimic, young Mathews polished his talents as principal comic of the York Company before making his London debut; despite his success with audiences, manager Tate Wilkinson advised the earnest performer he was "too tall for low comedy... one hiss would blow you off the stage!"

The Mail Coach Adventure (1808) was Mathews' first attempt — in the tradition of Foote and Dibdin — to venture outside the legitimate comedies in which he gained his reputation. The two-part show, with which he toured the provinces, featured his wife in a minor role; he later reworked it as a one-man "table entertainment." In the spring of 1818, he inaugurated a celebrated solo series of *At Homes* at London's Lyceum Theatre.

Charles Mathews, right, and four of his characterizations, as depicted by G.H. Harlow. 1814.

At home or abroad, Mathews enjoyed great popularity. When he toured the U.S. in 1822, the *Baltimore Patriot* enthused: "If the experiment had not been fully tried, it would be considered incredible, that any one man, by the variety of his tones... and the rich humor of his style and manner, could satisfy raised expectation, and keep his hearers either in a roar of applause, or in a state of tranquil pleasure."

An evening with Mathews began with two acts of monologues and songs, followed by a "monopolylogue" — a third-act multi-character farce in which the comedian essayed all the roles. Mathews often included imitations of well-known actors but, unlike Foote, his mimicry was absent of malice; if an imitation offended someone, he changed it.

Other solo performers of the nineteenth century included Moses Kean, who performed his *Evening Lounge* in London and the provinces; Miss Scott, who wrote and performed a one-woman show of recitations, imitations and songs at the Sans Pareil, which her father built for her; comedian Jack Bannister, who offered *Bannister's Budget*; Albert Smith, whose *Overland Mail* emulated Mathews' endeavors; and William Love, the so-called Dramatic Polyphonist, whose *Ventriloquial Entertainment* ran for decades.

Nineteenth century entertainers themselves have been a favorite subject of solo shows in recent years. Ben Kingsley followed his Oscar-winning film performance as Gandhi with a one-man portrayal of Shakespearean actor Edmund Kean; Frank Barrie has toured internationally as Kean's rival, William Charles Macready; and Constance Cummings has assumed the identity of actress Fanny Kemble.

Today in London's West End — where the regal Garrick Club preserves the last traces of an era when performing without a license was prohibited, and acting solo was a highly suspicious endeavor — entertainments with a cast of one are as popular as ever. Early in 1989, *Shirley Valentine* — a one-woman play about an unfulfilled Liverpool housewife starring Pauline Collins — won the prestigious Laurence Olivier award for comedy of the year.

Flights of FEAR and Fancy

Personality

The Art of Acting Solo

In the early years of the twentieth century, it was the job of a monologuist to stand in front of the curtain and talk, to facilitate changes of scenery. If he was a quick wit with a fast tongue, like Fred Allen, he might find himself pushed onstage to cover any crisis that arose. Today, the actor who masters the art of monologue to the extent Allen and his contemporaries did may well be the whole show, and often there is no scenery.

David Garrick, the greatest Shakespearean actor of his day, altered the text of *Hamlet* in 1772 to fatten the central role for himself. In 1899, William Gillette concocted a star vehicle from the stories of Conan Doyle, with himself as Sherlock Holmes. Today, they would no doubt dispense with their supporting ensembles and take to the stage alone.

When Sarah Bernhardt toured in the declining years of her career, she was but one element in the varied bill of fare on the vaudeville circuit; if she were making her farewell appearance now, it would probably be in the sole role of a show tailored to her talents — assuming she had the stamina.

"The whole thing has reached the proportions of a trend," Joseph Wood Krutch observed in *The Nation* in 1952. "Before long those two-character dramas which occasionally appear will seem positively cluttered, and some day we may have, by way of variety, that ultimate theatre proposed by an enthusiast in one of George Kaufman's comedies: 'No actors, no text, no audience; just scenery and critics.'"

Why the growing trend toward the one-person show in recent years? "Perhaps it has come about as a thrust against massness," suggests actress Pat Carroll, who toured in a one-woman play about expatriate American writer Gertrude Stein from 1979 to 1984. "We have become so conscious about being numbers — we're numbers everywhere. Acting solo has an appeal to me because it means one person can be on stage; it's not mandatory that groups make things happen," maintains Carroll. "I think it's important in this time of mass everything to realize that one person can have an effect on something."

Actors are especially conscious of being numbers. The Screen Actors Guild and Actors Equity, the stage actors' union, have a combined membership of approximately 100,000 members. With 85-90% of their number out of work, the one-man show has become a hedge against unemployment, a do-it-yourself pension plan and a ticket out of the rut.

Most entertainers content themselves with a life of hit-and-miss. "Even if we could do any damn thing we want to do, most of us wouldn't know what the hell to do. We hang around and wait for people to come to us with ideas and properties," says Carroll O'Connor, who once contemplated a one-man portrayal of Winston Churchill. "An actor might ruminate about what he'd like to do, but he doesn't plan things for himself unless he's also a manager and a producer. Chance is the biggest thing in an actor's life."

Moreso now than ever, performers are taking the reins

in their careers today and giving themselves the chance, lest opportunity fail to knock. Stars of international reputation and unknowns alike are increasingly performing solo. Many adapt or create their own entertainments; some commission others to write the script but elect to produce or direct the show themselves.

Acting solo is "the ultimate in egotism," asserts English actor Roy Dotrice, the one-man cast of plays about Churchill, Lincoln and seventeenth century gossip John Aubrey. "You require an exceedingly large ego to stand up there and think you can hold an audience's attention for a couple of hours. But there's nothing I know that's more satisfying... It's just you out there — no one else. There's no one to foul you up by stepping on your laugh or giving you the wrong cue."

Actors often talk about the *challenge* of doing a one-man show; rarely do they discuss the financial aspect. John Gielgud was characteristically blunt about such motives when he toured America with his Shakespeare recital, *Ages of Man* : "If you have anything to sell — talent or merchandise — there is always someone to buy it. I smelled this in England and I thought, 'If others can make money, I can, too.'"

One-person shows have taken on a myriad of forms over the years — impersonations, anthologies, adaptations, recitals and autobiographical monologues, among others. But not all can be conveniently labeled; some overlap and many others defy easy categorization or description, due to the very nature of theatre.

Literary and historical portrayals are by far the most

popular type of one-man show — at least with actors — as exemplified by Hal Holbrook's *Mark Twain Tonight!*, James Whitmore in *Will Rogers' U.S.A.* and as President Truman in *Give 'Em Hell, Harry*, and Julie Harris in *The Belle of Amherst* and *Brontë*.

Not all actors choose to portray such celebrated persons, however. *Journey Into the Whirlwind*, which had its U.S. premiere in 1987, features Rebecca Schull in her own adaptation of Soviet journalist Eugenia Ginsberg's harrowing account of life in a slave labor camp. "This was a remarkable woman — I want audiences to know her," reflects Schull. "And what happened didn't just happen to her, but to *millions* of others. It's important that people know these things exist."

The literary adaptation which does not result in a portrayal of the author is less commonly employed as a solo vehicle. Baruch Lumet acted in and directed various productions of S. Ansky's *The Dybbuk* before adapting the 30-character play into the one-man *Lumet's Legends*. Charles Marowitz served theatregoers *Tea With Lady Bracknell* by borrowing one of Oscar Wilde's most memorable characters, while Fred Curchack has twisted *The Tempest* into *Stuff As Dreams Are Made On*, in which he plays five roles.

Anthologies are eclectic in shape and form. Micheál Mac Liammóir paid tribute to Wilde in *The Importance of Being Oscar* without impersonating the author, while Fionnula Flanagan portrayed both real life and fictional females in *James Joyce's Women*. Oscar-winning actress Gale Sondergaard, who was blacklisted at the peak of her career, re-established herself with *Woman,* a solo show anthologizing Congreve, Ibsen and other playwrights.

Many shows made up of selections from multiple authors are little more than ill-conceived hodge podges, however. *The Square Root of Soul* — a 1977 evening of black poetry selected and performed by Adolph Caesar — was viewed as more of a collage than an anthology, which offered "a little something for everyone. And not much for anyone in particular," said *The New York Post.*

Readings and recitals are among the easiest and least expensive shows to produce. The late Charles Laughton assayed an evening of readings from the Bible to great success, revitalizing his career. Alec McCowen's more recent recital of *St. Mark's Gospel* has become a barometer by which other actors measure such efforts.

One-character plays, or monodramas, are generally the creation of playwrights rather than actors looking for a showcase vehicle. Many, however, are written with specific actors in mind — such as Jean Cocteau's *Le Fantome de Marseille* for Edith Piaf, *Krapp's Last Tape* by Samuel Beckett for Irish actor Patrick Magee, and *Diatribe of Love Against a Seated Man* by Gabriel García Márquez for Argentine actress Graciela Dufau.

Among the most engaging solos on the current scene is the contemporary show that presents a satiric look at life. It lacks the literary pedigree of other forms, but at its best has an immediacy and an energy that many more traditional programs lack; originality, in fact, is its hallmark. Comedians like Lily Tomlin and Eric Bogosian have graduated from nightclubs to legitimate theatrical venues with shows like *The Search for Signs of Intelligent Life in the Universe* and *Drinking in America.*

Satire and angst mix well in the solo form. Gina Wendkos' and Ellen Ratner's *Personality* is a young woman's search for personal identity, with a caustic edge that rivets the attention. Her face and body contorted into a caricature of a Jewish matron, a chain-smoking Ratner kvetches about her lazy 30-year-old daughter — "What man is going to want her?" After unloading on the audience, she puts out the cigarette, drops the accent and becomes the anxiety-ridden daughter, who alternately answers the pointed questions of an offstage psychiatrist and fields phone calls from her overbearing mother. The show has toured Europe, and has run for nearly two years at the Odyssey Theatre Ensemble in Los Angeles.

The autobiographical monologue is a more personal theatrical form that draws from within. Spalding Gray, who has elevated the genre to an art with *Swimming to Cambodia,* improvises his shows from an outline rather than work from a script, but does not deviate from the truth. "I'm interested in creative confession," says the self-described writer/actor/performer. "I would have made a great Catholic."

The semi-autobiographical fiction is a popular variation. One such show is Minnesota-based actress Chris Cinque's *Growing Up Queer in America,* which draws a parallel between her story of lesbian self-discovery and Dante's *Divine Comedy.* Kedric Robin Wolfe's solo shows are a mix of self-observation and storytelling based on personal experience — largely fictionalized and exaggerated.

British actor-writer David Cale's monologues have an emotional truth, which he insists, is "not the truth." There are elements drawn from his own life, but the stories are primarily fiction. *The Redthroats* — which tells the Dickensian misadventures of young Steven Weird — is simply "a piece of material. I'm just the actor performing it," says Cale, who has trouble with the labels people have put on his shows. They're part black comedy, part storytelling, he asserts, while "other parts are like spoken songs."

There are many shows which defy all classification. In the twenties, Angna Enters combined mime and dance to produce social commentary in the tradition of Greek and Roman mimes — in unique stage pieces that were difficult if not impossible to label. In the seventies, Italian actor-playwright Dario Fo created the controversial and popular theatrical spectacle, *Mistero buffo*, by distilling the traditions of Europe's medieval strolling players and the *commedia dell'arte* into a political and cultural attack on the Catholic church.

A more benign solo deriving from much the same roots is Geoff Hoyle's current *The Fool Show*, which begins with a brief lecture-demonstration on the history of fools, and co-mingles *commedia* antics with modern mime technique and new vaudeville. *Banjo Dancing* — which gives Stephen Wade a platform to relate tall tales, do the jig and plunk the banjo — is a vaudeville saturated in American folklore, but has roots that pre-date the *commedia* in the prehistoric art of storytelling. The show, which opened in 1979 at the Body Politic Theatre in Wade's native Chicago, played the Arena Stage in Washington, D.C., for nearly a decade.

One-person shows are as varied in purpose as they are in form. While Marcel Marceau's silent stories make eloquent remarks on the trials and tribulations of modern man, actresses like Whoopi Goldberg are using solo theatre to make verbal statements about the problems of women in today's society. Blacks, Asians, Jews and other minorities have used the solo as a forum for social comment and an opportunity to examine their heritage.

Goldberg's one-woman *Living on the Edge of Chaos* inspired actress Jude Narita to examine her Asian heritage via cultural stereotypes, and express "some outrage, some things that need to be said... in an artistic way." Narita's *Coming Into Passion/Song for a Sansei* consists of five vignettes which form a mosaic of the Asian woman in today's society, including a defiant teenage Sansei (third generation Japanese-American) who can't identify with Japan, a young Vietnamese prostitute and a Filipina mail-order bride.

Sansei, which originated at the Jazz Center of New York and ran 17 months at the tiny Fountain Theatre in Hollywood, traveled to Poland late in 1988 as part of a theatre project sponsored by the U.S. Information Agency. Despite reservations on the part of the actress and the producers, Narita's show drew strong response from Polish audiences, who identified with the universal predicaments of women.

Viveca Lindfors' *I Am a Woman*, which illuminated the female plight in an equally universal manner, began as an anthology of favorite monologues and poems and became a voyage of self-discovery. In the process of putting together the show, "I began to understand myself," Lindfors recalled in her autobiography. "We wanted it to be a journey of many women, not only mine, emotional as well as social. The first part of the journey took the woman into the past... the second part took the woman into the present, making her see the future, taking responsibility for it, politically and emotionally."

Sholem Aleichem and *Hannah Senesh* took their sole performers on journeys back to their roots. Veteran character actor Nehemiah Persoff has played virtually every nationality and every sort of character during his long career. Most of these roles denied, if not disguised, his Jewish identity. The Jerusalem-born actor acknowledged his heritage in 1971 when he chose the stories of Yiddish author Sholem Aleichem as the basis for a one-man show. His exploration of Aleichem's "little people," he observed, was "not just an obsession of sorts, it's a commitment and a challenge for me — as a man, as an artist and as a Jew."

Lori Wilner was unfamiliar with the tragic story of Hannah Senesh when playwright David Schechter first introduced her to the diaries of the young Hungarian Zionist who was tortured and executed by the Nazis. "I had never even heard of her," she concedes. "But when I got the diaries, I felt very connected and understood the parallels."

Wilner, who collaborated with Schechter on the project — and has portrayed the title role in *Hannah Senesh* since the show's debut in 1982 — emphasizes that the play is "not just another Holocaust story — it isn't a play about

Nehemiah Persoff's solo show affirmed his Jewish identity.

victimization. It's about fighting back, the importance of taking action and how one person can make a difference."

Bennet Guillory has been paying homage to such an individual for nearly a decade, as the star of *Paul Robeson* — a solo drama about the black actor-singer-political activist who put his career on the line by speaking out against oppression and racism. "Robeson talks about making choices, taking stands… he's someone who made a difference. And at the risk of patting myself on the back, I like to think that doing this play means I've made a difference too," says Guillory, who has toured with Philip Hayes Dean's drama on and off since 1980.

Many actors involved in solo theatre feel much the same way about their shows. Even if the program starts out as a device to keep them employed in lean periods or earn them an annuity, it often develops into something unexpected. When Barbara Rush began performing *A Woman of Independent Means* in 1984 at the Back Alley Theatre in Van Nuys, California, she thought it was just "a funny little project. I really didn't think it had much potential. I was only doing it one night a week… and just having some fun with it. Then I saw how everyone loved it, and I was amazed."

The play, adapted by Elizabeth Forsythe Hailey from her best-selling novel about the uneventful life of a well-heeled Texas matron — at Rush's suggestion — opened as a work-in-progress and ran for five months to sell-out crowds. "It's made me find my specialness," says Rush. "The play demands great vocal skills, certainly articulation… all these latent skills of mine are finally being used."

Public and critical response prompted the producers to skip the customary pre-Broadway circuit, only to make what Rush calls "a crucial mistake." Instead of keeping *Woman* simple, they dressed it up with superfluous backdrops and scenery.

"The temptation with a one-person show is to load it up, make it look gorgeous. But the production can get too big — it makes the one person on stage look small, and takes the focus away from them," asserts the show's stage manager, Scott Alsop, who says there is a negative attitude toward solo performers on The Great White Way: "It seems presumptuous to the Broadway critic for one person to come in and take over a theatre."

After *Woman* flopped in Manhattan's 900-seat Biltmore Theatre, it was redesigned with the intimacy of the first production and sent back out on the road. But Rush still found the program unnecessarily complicated. "The simpler a solo show is, the better it is for touring," maintains Alsop. "We have very intricate lighting, many changes of costume. The dresses are beautiful, but Barbara has to wear 75 pounds of layered costumes in the first act. Toward the end of the most recent tour, she began to wonder, 'Why can't we just put the lights on, do the show, and turn them off? Why can't I just do the whole thing in one dress?'"

Hailey's monodrama is one of dozens of one-person shows that have originated in the Los Angeles area and subsequently toured the country. The sheer number of actors in Southern California accounts for the multitude of such programs created and performed in the region. Solo shows seem to gravitate toward certain venues — the Odyssey Theatre and the Westwood Playhouse in Los Angeles, the Cherry Lane Theatre and the American Place Theatre in New York City, the Goodman Studio Theatre in Chicago, Ford's Theatre in Washington, D.C. — and the Edinburgh Theatre Festival in particular.

Commercial theatres are not the only venues open to those performing solo — particularly those appearing in the guise of historical figures. Nor are professional actors the only ones involved. Charles Brame, a retired history and political science teacher, has been presenting *The Living Lincoln* for over a decade to schoolchildren, senior citizens and service groups.

Prize-winning poet Robert Peters, a professor of English at the University of California at Irvine, finds the audience for poetry "so limited as to be almost non-existent." Seeking a broader audience for his work, he wrote a pair of one-person verse plays — *Mad King Ludwig of Bavaria* and *Ezerbet Bathory: The Blood Countess* — which he has performed at universities throughout the country.

Leia Morning, a scholar of British and American literature, performs her biographical sketches of Virginia Woolf, Jane Austen, Charlotte Brontë and others in museums, libraries and schools. "In a way, it's not acting," she says. "It's like really being someone else and allowing the genius of that person to operate through you."

Alec McCowen contemplated many avenues of approach before he devised a means of accomplishing just that with *St. Mark's Gospel*. After he rejected the idea of *playing* the enlightened author, "I decided that I would simply enter with my copy of St. Mark, put it on the table, take off my jacket and tell the story — as if it had just been told to me."

When the classically-trained British actor first turned to the Gospels to select the text for his recital, he rejected John, Matthew and Luke before choosing Mark. Although

ON STAGE

MARYMOUNT MANHATTAN THEATRE

ST. MARK'S GOSPEL

Alec McCowen in "the strangest adventure of my life."

McCowen felt Mark's Gospel had "extraordinary theatrical shape," he feared speaking it on a stage might be dull, and worried whether he would have the energy to sustain such an endeavor.

It took the actor 16 months to learn the lines; only then did he fully understand them, and appreciate the constant repetition of Mark's prosaic phrasing ("He said unto them...") McCowen then recorded his recitation of the entire Gospel, with startling results. "I found it impossible to listen to myself," he conceded. "It was formal, boring, lifeless, monotonous..."

Even after the first performance late in 1977, McCowen wondered why he had gone to the trouble of learning the lines, and whether in fact his performance wasn't an act of indulgence. "Of course you had to learn it!" a chaplain assured him. "Learning it makes it an act of faith." The recital went on to become one of the most successful solo programs of recent years.

Jascha Heifetz once said an artist must have "the nerves of a bullfighter, the vitality of a night-club hostess and the concentration of a Buddhist monk." As Alec McCowen and his colleagues would attest, these same qualities had best be tucked securely in the baggage trunk of any actor contemplating a one-man show.

The Queen and her Disciples

She was the much emulated but unrivaled "queen of one-woman theatre" for over four decades. She was described through the years as a monologuist, a mimic, an impersonator, a *diseuse* — but the title Ruth Draper herself preferred was "character actress."

She was a multilingual performer who traveled to almost every corner of the world with a collection of original sketches. She won the loyalty of the public, the patronage of royalty and the admiration of celebrated actors; she inspired such noted solo entertainers as Cornelia Otis Skinner, Joyce Grenfell and Lily Tomlin to follow the singular path she trod.

Draper (1884-1956) could portray beggars and society ladies with equal credibility. From starving waif to giddy debutante, Balkan peasant to French dressmaker, her characterizations were true to life. Her Scottish immigrant at Ellis Island was no less authentic than her temperamental Polish actress or her New York matron at an Italian lesson, or her portrait of a rural Irish woman recalling the death of her only son.

She accomplished her magic with the slightest of costumes and the simplest of props — a shawl, an occasional hat or cloak, a handbag or an umbrella. The stage was

Opposite: Ruth Draper in *A Scottish Immigrant at Ellis Island*, as seen by John Singer Sargent. 1914.

adorned by no more than a chair or table; it was often bare of all furniture.

"It is the audience who must supply the imagination," Draper told an interviewer. "What is really important is not to put anything 'over,' but to bring the audience up onto the stage and into the scene with you. It is they who must give you even more than you give them in the way of imagination and creative power."

The self-trained actress expected theatregoers to participate but conceded that it was a lot to ask of modern audiences, their creativity deadened by movies and television. She herself had an abundant supply. "What I had as a child I've never lost — the child's ability to *pretend:* to *be* what he imagines he is. If you give yourself completely to what you pretend you are, you will convince other people it exists, and only then."

Draper, a native of New York City, began to cultivate an ability for mimicry as a youngster; a diminutive Jewish tailor employed by her mother became the unsuspecting subject of her first study. The characterizations she drew for the amusement of family and friends soon brought requests for benefits and recitals in private homes.

She made her stage debut in 1916 when Marie Tempest saw her sketches, and offered her a small role in a broad farce called *A Lady's Name*. The following year Draper staged a program consisting of Strindberg's two-character one-act, *The Stronger*, and two pieces of her own — *An Old Story*, a "pantomime in three scenes," and *The Actress*, a "solo play." Critics labeled it "ill-advised" and "singularly misguided and tedious." Apart from a few all-star benefits,

Ruth Draper relaxes backstage in Brighton, England, on her 1951 tour of the British Isles. Her popularity in the U.K. was unsurpassed.

she performed by herself — in material entirely her own — for the remainder of her career.

Draper was the consummate professional by the time she gave her first one-woman show in a public theatre. On January 29, 1920, she presented a two-hour program of character sketches — or "monos," as she called them — at Aeolian Hall in London.

"Her observation is almost wickedly keen, her expression of it is pointed and polished till it is as clear and bright as a diamond," remarked the *Times* reviewer. The sentiment was to be echoed by critics and audiences for the next three decades — particularly in England where she was even more warmly received than America.

At the outset of her career, Draper was often compared with British monologuist Beatrice Herford (1868-1952). To Herford's "incomparable wit and finesse, [Draper] has always added a significant touch of her own," wrote *The New York Times'* John Corbin in 1923. "Miss Herford's observation inclines to the impish and malicious... Miss Draper has from the start added a touch of sentiment which at times declines upon sentimentality, but which at its best is warmly sympathetic and humanly nourishing."

It was the contrast in her material that distinguished Draper not only from Herford — whose comedy monologues were a decisive influence — but from those who followed her as well. "Few were to venture into Ruth's essays in starker drama and realism," stated biographer Morton D. Zabel.

The dramatic recitation, popularized by Charles Dickens in the Victorian era, had fallen into disrepute on the vaudeville and Chatauqua circuits by the time Draper appeared on the scene, as Zabel pointed out in *The Art of Ruth Draper*. "She must have begun her career convinced that something new in the way of taste, skill and refinement was needed to make a serious art of it," he noted. While a few of Draper's portraits were in the Dickensian tradition, he observed, "most of her sketches are explicit in their repudiation of exaggerated caricature and melodrama."

Draper also set herself apart from her predecessors by developing her character sketches into short plays. In *Three Women and Mr. Clifford*, she portrayed a businessman's secretary in the first act, his wife in the second act and his mistress in the third. In the three acts of *Three Breakfasts* she depicted the history of a marriage, as an eager young bride turned bored society matron, and then a frail but happy old lady. Draper could reportedly alter her age, her figure and her physiogamy as needed.

The sketches, regardless of length, were not written out. Draper — who always rehearsed in front of a mirror — carried them in her memory and never used scripts or prompt books. The monologues changed in phrasing and detail over the years, as she performed them; she was "never satisfied with a final form." With two exceptions, they were based not on actual incidents or people but fabricated from her imagination.

The key element in her work was simplicity. Her sketches and playlets were not unique in situation, nor were they wildly inventive in the treatment of their subjects. "Their appeal was the appeal of the familiar, the casual, the average, and the recognizable," asserted Zabel.

The actress broke all records for solo performances during the 1928-29 season, at the Comedy Theatre in New

York; opening on Christmas night, she put on eight shows a week for 19 weeks. The demand for tickets was so great the following season, she performed on the same stage for 20 continuous weeks. Draper was as popular with the crowned heads of Europe as she was with the common man; in 1951 she was made a Commander of the British Empire. The royalty of her own profession were equally awestruck. "Her authority and her concentration were absolute," observed John Gielgud. "How swiftly she transformed that stage into her own extraordinary world, transporting us to other places, other countries... creating in each of those imagined settings a single dominant character and then seeming to surround herself, as and when she needed them, with an attendant crowd of minor figures."

When critic Kenneth Tynan saw Draper for the first time in 1952, he discovered "she had all but ruined the pleasures of normal playgoing [for many in the audience] since her large supporting cast, which exists only at her fingertips, is so much more satisfactory than any which makes the vulgar mistake of being visible." He concluded that Draper's one-woman performance was "the best and most modern group acting" he had ever seen.

Brooks Atkinson found her "entirely credible" in 1956 when the 72-year-old actress portrayed the young girl of *In a Railway Station on the Western Plains* — a sketch she had offered in her first New York stage solo 35 years earlier. His glowing *New York Times* review of her Christmas night performance pointed out with some urgency that she was appearing at the Playhouse Theatre for "a limited engagement." Five days later, Draper died in her sleep.

If not for the foresight of her producers, Charles Bowden and Richard Barr, Draper's work would have vanished with her. In 1955-56 she recorded a number of her monologues for RCA Victor. Because she was self-conscious in front of the microphones, the recordings had to be made surreptitiously during "warmup time," prior to the scheduled sessions.

Cornelia Otis Skinner (1901-1979), who gave her first one-woman show in 1928, was among the most successful of Draper's admirers and followers. As Draper had been compared to Beatrice Herford, Skinner was invariably compared with Draper. Entertainer Pat Carroll, who saw both performers as a child, recently observed, "Miss Skinner had a terrific personality, a theatrical personality, but Miss Draper was a real actress... the difference between maybe Sarah Bernhardt and Eleanora Duse."

Skinner — the Chicago-born daughter of renowned actor-manager Otis Skinner — began with programs of solo sketches not unlike Draper's. She soon distinguished herself by creating a series of elaborate costume dramas, notably *The Wives of Henry VIII*. Skinner further distanced herself from her illustrious predecessor in 1937 with *Edna His Wife*, a full-length adaptation of a bestselling novel.

The play, in which Skinner portrayed three generations of women, was acclaimed as a "tour de force" by some, but received less appreciatively by others. "A woman talking steadily for two hours... is not my idea of entertainment, whether in the theatre or in private," declared theatre critic George Jean Nathan. "She is not an actress. She is rather simply the impersonator of and commentator on an actress."

Undaunted, Skinner went on to create the even more

Cornelia Otis Skinner, above, circa 1950;
Joyce Grenfell in 1954-55 revue.

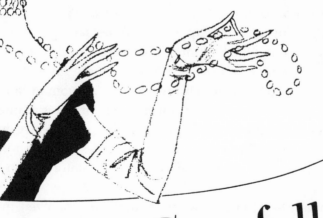

Joyce Grenfell
Requests The Pleasure...

elaborate *Paris '90*, "a monodrama in 14 scenes." Unlike Draper, however, she enjoyed the company of other actors on stage, and appeared in a number of plays — notably Shaw's *Candida* and her own comedy of manners, *The Pleasure of His Company*. She was also a celebrated author and an essayist of some note.

She continued to perform the solo programs, largely for women's clubs, but admitted she "always chafed at the platform" and finally, after 40 years, that she was "fed up with the extracurricular things" — the early morning shows, the obligatory luncheons and the idiotic questions ("Favorite monologue? Whichever one happened to have gone best at that performance.")

"I don't look back on them on them with rapture," Skinner said of the club engagements, for which she received "a rousing $150-200" when she started, and $1,200-1,500 in the mid-sixties when she tired of them. "I'm a pro and I don't feel that they constitute a pro audience." Her father, a great admirer of Draper, felt his daughter's monologues were "her medium" — but Skinner looked upon them as "something for me to go back to between jobs."

Draper, whose one-woman shows were her only "job," was uncomfortable in the presence of other solo entertainers like Skinner, and rarely went to see them. British comedienne Joyce Grenfell (1910-1979), a lifelong devotee of her work, asked Draper for advice at the start of her own career — only to discover that "she thought I was out to compete with her. I could not have done so if I tried," said Grenfell. "It was like a goddess fearing a mortal. There was no possible threat."

A native of London whose father was a distant cousin of Draper's, Grenfell grew up watching — and worshipping — the preeminent solo performer. She was always quick to acknowledge Draper as the inspiration for her monologues. "I would not have thought of trying to do anything so peculiar unless I had seen her do it first," she noted in her autobiography.

"From the beginning I was conscious that whatever I wrote should be kept well away from Ruth's territory — for instance, her portrayals of upper-class English women... by the time I had begun to write [monologues], these women were already a little out of date; that simplified any temptations I might have had to quarry where she had already mined."

Instead, she used her tall, thin, long-legged torso, her rubbery face and its toothy grin, an inimitable voice and a razor-sharp ear for dialects to create a gallery of eccentrics and gargoyles: a dainty lecturer who slid her vowel sounds; the intellectual vice chancellor's wife with the crisp tongue; and most memorably, the nursery schoolteacher with the utter lack of confidence.

Grenfell was a newspaper columnist in 1939 when a BBC writer asked her to do one of her monologues at a party; as a result, she was asked to perform two sketches in *The Little Revue*. She was an immediate success. Her comedy sketches and songs were subsequently featured in such revues as Noël Coward's *Sigh No More, Tuppence Colored* and *Penny Plain;* she was also heard on radio and seen in such films as *The Belles of St. Trinians*.

She did not appear in a show of her own until 1954, when she opened in *Joyce Grenfell Requests the Pleasure*.

While the revue — for which she wrote the book and lyrics — featured a trio of dancers, it was essentially an evening of monologues and songs built around her talents. She then toured as a solo performer, accompanied only by a pianist, for the remainder of her career.

Despite their travels to the far flung edges of the globe, neither Grenfell nor Draper enjoyed the audiences that have greeted Lily Tomlin in recent years. Nor did either have the vast exposure afforded to her by hit movies and TV shows that has resulted in sell-out crowds wherever Tomlin has presented her unique one-woman entertainments.

Tomlin was performing impressions in a coffeehouse in her native Detroit when a patron's incidental remark sent her in search of the recordings Draper had made with grudging reluctance. She came away "totally inspired" by the legendary monologuist and her art form. "There's such a richness of language and character and humor and humanity and, I guess, artistry," marvels Tomlin. "Artistry is the word."

Cabaret audiences were familiar with her bizarre routines — like tap-dancing in her barefeet — before Tomlin graduated to television, gracing *The Garry Moore Show* with her comic monologues. A three-year stint on the frantically-paced *Rowan & Martin's Laugh-In*, beginning in 1969, brought her into her own and introduced two hugely popular characterizations: Edith Ann, the precocious five-year-old brat, and Ernestine, the nasal telephone operator with the arrogant manner ("Is this the party to whom I am speaking?")

Tomlin starred in four Emmy-winning TV specials before attempting her first one-woman Broadway show in

Lily Tomlin carries on the traditions of Ruth Draper.

1977. *Appearing Nitely* showcased her chameleon-like ability with a wildly inventive parade of characters, and won a Tony award.

Unlike Draper, Skinner and Grenfell, Tomlin is not the principal creator of her solo material. The writer who gives voice to many of the zany personas is longtime collaborator Jane Wagner, who has helped Tomlin to expand her talents. "She always felt safer doing characters she knew, that were somehow connected to her childhood," says Wagner. "I told her that to grow, she had to try out new characters."

Tomlin — who says she identifies with all the personas she plays — excluded Ernestine and Edith Ann from the cast of *The Search for Signs of Intelligent Life in the Universe*, in favor of more contemporary characters like punk rocker Agnes Angst. Unlike *Appearing Nitely*, the second solo show — which she began touring early in 1985 — is more than a collection of self-contained skits; from Lynn, the exasperated feminist, to Trudy, the nutty bag lady who observes that reality "is nothing but a collective hunch," each character is part of a complex whole.

"It's always been my intention in my work to try to give

some order to this planet, and I think this has been most fully realized in this show... I like to think of the show as *prismatic*. We would like everybody [in the audience] to identify with everybody else, to stop thinking in definitive or rigid ways about things and about people, and to understand that we are all in this cosmic soup together," says the 50-year-old comedienne.

"It's no longer enough to be funny or sad," explains Wagner, who considers her pungent social commentary a *play*. "It's not just the typical monologue form," says the writer-director, despite the absence of props, scenery or costume changes in *Search for Signs*. "We have nothing to hide behind but each other. When you deal with an expository form like this you have nothing to shield you. There's just Lily and the material. Every word becomes a delicate choice because every word is so obvious... when there is one person up there performing, what else do you have to go on but words?"

The tradition of Ruth Draper survives not only in the person of Lily Tomlin today, but in her own words. Her recordings are now available on a series of Spoken Arts audio cassettes. Her monologues are also being kept alive by composer Lee Hoiby, who turned *The Italian Lesson* into a *scena* for Jean Stapleton, and by actress Patrizia Norcia, who has been studying Draper's work for years and can perform several hours of it. Maureen Lipman is similarly introducing new audiences to Joyce Grenfell with *Re:Joyce*, a delicious one-woman tribute to one of Draper's most accomplished disciples.

BONFILS THEATRE & SOL HUROK

present

EMLYN WILLIAMS as CHARLES DICKENS

In Person

On January 28, 1952, Charles Dickens glided onto the stage of the Plymouth Theatre in Boston, Massachusetts, with the assurance of a matinee idol. He bowed stiffly, removed his white gloves, took a sip of water and thumbed the pages of a dusty volume on his burgundy velvet lectern — then wrapped his tongue around the melodramatic prose, lifted it from the printed page and spewed it at the audience. In due course he mimicked a passel of characters from his novels and stories, each distinct in voice, manner and gesture, shifting from one to another with remarkable speed. Even more remarkable was the fact that he had been dead since 1870.

The dignified gentleman who appeared that winter night in Victorian evening clothes was not the ghost of the nineteenth century English author but a reincarnation. From the red geranium in the lapel of his frock coat, to the drooping mustache and neatly parted chin whiskers, he was every inch the embodiment of Dickens.

Emlyn Williams (1905-1987) was the son of a Welsh coal miner who, like the famed novelist, endured a penurious childhood. Both enjoyed literary success in their mid-twenties, Dickens with *Pickwick Papers*, Williams as a playwright with *A Murder Has Been Arranged*. But where Dickens was a frustrated actor who dabbled in amateur theatricals, Williams was a consummate professional who won acclaim for performing in his own plays — as a psychotic killer in *Night*

Must Fall and a near illiterate-turned-scholar in his celebrated autobiographical work, *The Corn is Green*.

In 1950 Williams hit upon the idea for a one-man show
while reading an account of Dickens' tours of Britain and
America. Dickens had enjoyed almost unprecedented adu-
lation when he embarked on a series of public readings in
his later years, with an arduous itinerary that earned him a
sizable fortune but hastened his death.

The tours that killed Dickens gave birth to a whole new
career for Williams. At the outset, he later recalled, "It was
terribly tentative, because I didn't know if I could last a
whole evening." Despite his initial skepticism the actor
toured intermittently in *Emlyn Williams as Charles Dickens*
for over 35 years, taking the show throughout Europe and
the United States, and on to South America, South Africa,
Australia and the Soviet Union.

Although Williams was something of a novelty when
he first donned Dickens' white gloves and split beard in the
early nineteen fifties, actors working alone on stage were
commonplace. Ruth Draper had been performing original
monologues for over three decades; more recently, Charles
Laughton, Claude Rains and John Carradine had each presented readings from the classics. But few had attempted
anything as inventive as the Welsh actor-playwright who
merged identities with Dickens.

Modeling his grandiloquent delivery after the author's,
Williams would stand almost motionless at the rostrum,
employing faint smiles, raised eyebrows and minimal gestures, "playing the characters as I imagine Dickens would

have played them — playing them through him." The actor went to extraordinary lengths to satisfy himself that he was being true to Dickens; he was so obsessed with authenticity that he borrowed the lectern Dickens himself designed and used, from a London museum, and had it replicated for his show.

Williams created three additional one-man entertainments, including the much heralded *Dylan Thomas Growing Up*. He personally encouraged a number of actors to put together their own solo programs and inspired several others to perform in the guise of literary and historical figures.

The one-man show — especially the famous personage come back to life — gained phenomenal popularity with actors and audiences alike when Hal Holbrook won the Tony Award for his portrayal of Mark Twain in 1966. In addition to Twain, such incisive writers as H.L. Mencken, Alexander Woollcott and Damon Runyon have been impersonated on the stage in recent years. Actor-writer Paul Shyre, who adapted and directed *Will Rogers' U.S.A.* for James Whitmore, portrayed Mencken, the celebrated curmudgeon, in his own *Blasts and Bravos*. Peter Boyden interpreted Woollcott in Howard Teichmann's *Smart Aleck* and John Martello recreated *Damon Runyon's Broadway*.

On the distaff side, Zoe Caldwell put the controversial Lillian Hellman back on the witness stand in William Luce's *Lillian*. Celeste Holm played journalist Janet Flanner in Shyre's *Paris Was Yesterday*, while Elizabeth Van Dyke portrayed playwright Lorraine Hansberry in *Love to All, Lorraine*. There have been numerous attempts at Dorothy

"GORGEOUS!"
- Clive Barnes, N.Y. Times

"IRRESISTIBLE!"
- Doug Watt, Daily News

"MENCKEN LIVES!"
- Martin Gottfried, N.Y. POST

Edgar Lansbury, Joseph Beruh and Torquay Company
present

PAUL SHYRE
in

BLASTS AND BRAVOS:
an evening with H.L.Mencken

Adapted by
PAUL SHYRE

Production Designed by
ELDON ELDER

CHERRY LANE THEATRE 38 COMMERCE ST.

Caricature by Al Hirschfeld

H.L. Mencken — who has been described by Alastair Cooke as "the master craftsman of daily journalism in the twentieth century" — was portrayed by Paul Shyre in his 1975 adaptation of the newspaperman's work.

Parker, a favorite of both amateur and professional actors.

Historical figures hold equal fascination. Henry Fonda electrified audiences as *Clarence Darrow* while Eileen Heckart captured the spirit of a great first lady in *Eleanor*. More recently, Linda Hunt portrayed concentration camp survivor Annulla Allen in Emily Mann's *Annulla*, which started as an oral history project. Playwright Donald Freed has worked against expectations to evoke pity for Richard Nixon in *Secret Honor* — as played by Philip Baker Hall — and demythologize turn-of-the-century Mexican hero Pancho Villa.

Overcoming audience preconceptions has been a persistent problem for James Whitmore over the years. The actor had a hard time convincing people that Teddy Roosevelt could be gentle, Will Rogers could be serious or Harry Truman could possess a sense of humor. "Audiences insist on the cliche, and with Teddy it's the bully who charged up San Juan Hill," he told an interviewer while touring in Jerome Alden's *Bully*. Similarly, Truman didn't have a sense of humor in public. But during research for *Give 'Em Hell, Harry*, said Whitmore, "we found that in private he was very funny, indeed."

The actor himself had preconceived notions about Rogers before he began working on *Will Rogers' U.S.A.* "I expected the worst from that one," conceded Whitmore. "I hadn't found the script that good or amusing and I was very worried — until I found that Rogers performs better than he reads." Whitmore entered the stage not as Rogers but as Whitmore in the first of his three solo shows, which he began touring early in 1970. "If you look up Will Rogers in your encyclopedia... you'll find the following short note," he told audiences, proceeding to read the entry. He then expanded on the subject as he doffed his coat and tie, took a rope in hand, pushed a hat on his head, and began to chew a wad of gum. Finally, as his voice took on a folksy twang, he dropped into a bowlegged stance and grinned the familiar Rogers grin — to a roar of approval.

Producer George Spota created the introductory device for Henry Fonda, who was originally to have played the role, when Fonda worried that audiences would not accept him as Rogers. Whitmore was no less anxious about his ability to win the audience over. "I have great trepidation trying to create what was so well known and so well liked. I'm not an impressionist... even with Rogers, I didn't do an imitation. The main thing I strive for is to get the fundamental man, to recreate the rhythmic patterns. That's more important than doing an imitation," said Whitmore.

"I don't know how I get into these things," the veteran actor told *The New York Times*. "I don't look like any of those guys. Nor do I try to mimic at all — simply because I can't do it. I don't wear makeup either, because I'm allergic to it. About all I do is cut my hair differently." Whitmore's acclaimed portrayals of Rogers, Truman and Roosevelt were far from definitive, he maintained. "They can't be. You just hope to be able to grasp the hem of the garment, so to speak, to give a sense of the man you're dealing with."

Unlike their eighteenth century predecessors — who were limited in part by public tastes — most of today's solo performers disdain mimicry. Where Samuel Foote and his contemporaries honed their imitations razor sharp, today's

Courtesy of George Spota

Will Rogers' U.S.A. — an election year favorite — starred James Whitmore as the legendary American humorist who observed that political parties "are both good and bad… good when they're out and bad when they're in."

actors usually attempt expressionistic portraits of their subjects; their performances, in the main, are far more than
skin-deep impersonations.

Roy Dotrice's makeup for *Churchill* consisted of seven
pliable pieces to round out his face, and a dental appliance
which pushed out his lower lip and helped him with the
statesman's slur. Despite such efforts, the English actor
conceded, "I think it would be a terrible impertinence to
imitate him literally — and it might not be good theatre,
either, since he tended to drop his voice at the end of his
sentences... which is just what you learn not to do as an
actor."

Philip Baker Hall read Richard Nixon's memoirs during preparation for *Secret Honor*, but did not use newsreel
footage or audio tapes for research, as Whitmore had for
Truman. "I didn't want to do an imitation, I didn't want to
do Nixon mannerisms; that would intrude on what I was
trying to do. I was dealing with the character Donald Freed
wrote, who was not the real Nixon," says Hall, who played
the chief executive as a neurotic man coming apart at the
seams. The result, says Julie Harris, was "a masterful performance."

Freed, an investigative reporter who was once on
Nixon's "enemies list," collaborated on the play with Arnold Stone, an attorney who worked with the U.S. Department of Justice. Their depiction of a suicidal, self-pitying
Nixon is one of the few biographical dramas ever based on
a living personality. *Secret Honor*, which debuted at the Los
Angeles Actors' Theatre in 1983, is also one of the most
provocative and controversial one-man shows ever
mounted.

Photo by Demetrios Demetroupolous

Philip Baker Hall's 1983 characterization of Nixon in *Secret Honor* was based solely on his imagination; James Whitmore studied films, still photos and audio tapes to recreate Truman in his 1975 *Give 'Em Hell, Harry.*

Photo by Marque Neal Jr.

Philip Hayes Dean's *Paul Robeson* stirred even greater controversy when first produced in 1978, with James Earl Jones as the outspoken entertainer who had died just two years earlier. Robeson's son objected so strongly to the play, he collected signatures of black notables and ran an ad in *Variety* calling it "a pernicious perversion of the essence of Paul Robeson." When the play was revived on Broadway in 1988, Robeson Jr. asserted, "I still think that in its lines the play was about someone else, not my father... it leaves out much that was not just important but essential."

Juni Dahr, a member of the National Theatre of Norway, chose Joan of Arc as the subject of a recent solo portrayal not because she was a heroine, but because Dahr wanted to explore her human side. "She's not heroic. She was not a saint. She was not an angel. She had doubts. She's *real*," says the actress. "What does it mean when you begin to believe in something bigger than you? I wanted to find out." In researching *Joan of Arc: Vision Through Fire*, Dahr and director John Morrow used original texts and actual transcripts from Joan's trials — and ended up with a character far more complex than the one depicted by Shaw.

Some solo entertainments are plays — they not only have character development, they have plot, emotional logic, continuity and conflict. *Mark Twain Tonight!* is no less entertaining than *The Belle of Amherst*, but it more closely resembles a vaudeville turn than a play. Hal Holbrook himself conceded in a 1959 program note, "I have dearly wanted to get as much of Mark Twain on the stage as I can. But I cannot turn him completely inside out, as a playwright would be able to do, because I am portraying Twain as a lecturer and he did not cry in public."

Joel Kimmel's *At Wit's End* — in which Stan Freeman is currently touring as pianist and humorist Oscar Levant — is advertised as "a play with music." It is nothing of the kind. It is part cabaret, part monologue, long on anecdotes, short on development and continuity. Freeman's piano technique is dazzling; Levant's one-liners are some of the funniest ever written or spoken — to wit, "I either have bronchitis, or a chest full of congealed emotions." But when Freeman/Levant prefaces the wisecracks with, "I once said about so-and-so..." instead of delivering them in present tense, the show becomes a museum piece.

Seizing the audience's attention in a one-person biographical drama — and holding onto it — is far more difficult than in a multi-character play. Setting the stage is crucial, if the solo show is to succeed. Henry Fonda, as David Rintels' *Clarence Darrow,* began by reminiscing about his father's humiliating attempt to witness a public execution, and then about the hottest summer day of his childhood, on which he hoed potatoes — "and after I had worked hard for a few hours, I ran away from that hard work, went into the practice of law, and have not done any work since."

Donald Freed's *Villa,* set in a deserted park, opened on a stone statue of the legendary Mexican general that came to life in the person of scholar-actor Julio Medina. The imaginative premise had the statue speaking to the audience in the context of a dream, or "possibly the audience's nightmare after eating a Mexican meal," observed Freed.

Willard Simms' *Einstein: The Man Behind the Genius* — in which Larry Gelman has toured for several years — begins with the famed mathematician at the blackboard in his Princeton University study, back to the audience: "My friends! I was so involved in my work I did not hear you come in." Herbert Mitgang opened *Mister Lincoln* with what *The New York Times* called "a banal fiction" — the president sitting in his box at Ford's Theatre, describing his murder and telling the audience how "my life passed before my dying brain."

Recreating the lives of famous people, and making them live for today's audiences, often leads to contrived dramatic situations. Samuel Gallu's *Churchill* — which began with Sir Winston on the toilet, cigar in one hand and red telephone in the other, talking to President Roosevelt — struck at least one critic as a series of contrivances. "The phone is the first indication of what is to be a nagging failure of Gallu's imagination," observed Jack Viertel of *The Los Angeles Herald Examiner.* "This is a Churchill who needs props. If a door isn't knocked on or a phone doesn't ring or an intercom doesn't buzz, he is all but helpless on stage... The one-man show needs more of a plan."

In the course of Gallu's ingenious "political cabaret," *Give 'Em Hell, Harry!,* James Whitmore's Harry Truman casually noticed a newspaper item about Herbert Hoover being in town, called his hotel and invited the former president to the White House; minutes later, he shook hands with the invisible Hoover and initiated a brief chat with him in the Oval Office. Later still, he conversed with the ghost of Franklin Roosevelt, represented by an empty chair in a spotlight.

Whitmore's dynamic performance and Peter Hunt's imaginative direction went a long way toward making such seemingly artificial moments work. Less well devised enterprises like Bill Studdiford's *Byron in Hell* — in which Ian Frost has been touring as the seventeenth century poet for five years — virtually reek with contrivances. The dramatist has set his subject in purgatory, flashing lights and all, and surrounded him with portraits of friends, lovers and wives; the stage is so cluttered with canvases Frost/Byron can scarcely move around, nor can he talk about anyone without displaying their picture.

Drama critic and radio personality Alexander Woollcott, who called himself "a man of impeccable taste," was similarly ill served by Howard Teichmann, in the opinion of some critics. "*Smart Aleck* has the faults common to one-man shows about famous artists: too much narrative and not enough action; too much emphasis on the superficial celebrity side of the subject's life and not enough on the substance of his work and thought; a too-hasty snatching at over-simplified 'psychological' explanations," ventured Michael Feingold of *The Village Voice.*

While some critics have declared a bias against solo portrayals, others, like Dan Sullivan of *The Los Angeles Times,* have professed admiration for the genre. "Whatever such an evening may lack in shape, it will at least be about someone worth paying attention to, someone who made a difference... [these shows] leave you feeling somewhat better about our chances for survival. They remind us that we do, occasionally, come up with a winner," Sullivan has written.

"We want to hear about people who thought they could do something about this world they never made. These shows provide that kind of hope. If a Clarence Darrow could squeeze justice from the courts; if a Will Rogers could blow the stage smoke away from Government and expose the very ordinary people hiding there; if a Harry Truman could tell the Klu Klux Klan where to put it... maybe there's a chance for us. Even if the message doesn't take," observed Sullivan, "one leaves this type of evening feeling more nourished than is often the case of theatre of fiction."

Roy Dotrice is equally enamored of one-man biographical dramas. The actor was more in love with the idea for *Mister Lincoln* than he was with Herbert Mitgang's script but quickly became obsessed with the role, for which he read more than 40 books. "It would never do for an Englishman to play Lincoln in the States," he decided at the outset. "But it went so well in Canada that I thought I would try Washington... and see." The show was a hit when it played Ford's Theatre early in 1979, but Dotrice was assassinated by critics when he took it to Broadway the following year, for being "too English and too short."

It was not the first time the esteemed actor — a veteran of the Royal Shakespeare Company — had lost his footing on American soil. *Brief Lives,* in which he played seventeenth century gossip and antiquary John Aubrey, ran for a record-breaking 1700 performances — including 213 at the Criterion Theatre in London; it closed after 16 perform-ances on Broadway. It was an expensive flop, too, losing over $100,000.

Patrick Garland's *Brief Lives* was not only one of the costliest one-man shows ever mounted — the set was clut-tered with over 2,000 antiquarian objects — its subject was one of the most obscure. "Other actors said I was crazy, that nobody had heard of Aubrey," recalled Dotrice. The actor himself "like most Englishmen" was unfamiliar with Aubrey until he portrayed him in the 1964 Shakespeare quadracentennial at Stratford.

What is required to pull off such an effort, Dotrice has said, "is a certain amount of classical training, and a bit of the vaudeville comedian in you. When an audience sees an ordinary play, they're at a keyhole watching the drama unfold. But it's a totally different situation when a guy gets there and says, I'm Charles Dickens or Mark Twain or whatever. That's direct communication."

For some actors, the intimacy is almost too direct. Col-leen Dewhurst was admittedly looking for an annuity when she decided to portray the widow of Eugene O'Neill, with whose work she is so strongly identified. But when the actress took on the burden of performing Barbara Gelb's *My Gene* in 1987, she found herself enmeshed in the worst professional experience of her career. "Not the worst in terms of working but the worst in terms of the sheer un-adulterated tension and fear," she conceded at the time. "After this, it's going to be so-o-o-o exciting to look across a

ROY DOTRICE

in **Brief Lives**

Criterion
THEATRE

Playbill
PROGRAMME 1ᵖ

Roy Dotrice gave scholar John Aubrey "the recognition that eluded him… three centuries later" in his long-running *Brief Lives*.

stage and see another actor going, 'And then what happened?'"

Many performers are scared half to death by the prospects of facing an audience on their own — which is exactly the reason some take the plunge into solo theatre — while others are seemingly undaunted by the challenge. To the personalities they resurrect there appears no end. George C. Scott is filling the shoes of Henry Fonda, in the role of Clarence Darrow. Cloris Leachman is depicting painter Grandma Moses. Pat Hingle is reinventing the life of Thomas Edison. Harold Gould is analyzing the persona of Sigmund Freud. William Windom continues to milk the wit and wisdom of James Thurber, as he has for more than a decade, while Hal Holbrook sails through his 36th year as Twain — matching the endurance record of Emlyn Williams as Dickens.

Despite the abundance of one-person shows on the boards, those who succeed in solo portrayals of literary or historical figures are few, says producer George Spota — a longtime proponent of biographical drama, who is responsible for *Will Rogers' U.S.A.*, *Bully* and *Eleanor*. "Ninety-five percent of all professionals will walk away from a one-man show at the last minute," he asserts, "because four basic qualities are needed to pull it off... consummate artistry, intellectual clarity, a sense of the social ramifications of their character, and an ego flexible enough to let them get under their character's skin." Lacking any of these qualities, says Spota, "the actor is liable to have a recurrent dream of being naked before an audience with two hours to kill."

Will the Real Mark Twain Please Stand Up?

"Ladies and gentlemen... Chaucer is dead," drawls the man in the white linen suit. He clears his throat and peers at the audience. "Chaucer is dead... Milton is dead... and I'm not feeling too good myself," he stammers, taking a leisurely puff on his cigar. An elder statesman of comedy like George Burns might get a lot of mileage out of such material; Mark Twain, who was smoking cigars long before Burns was born, and who wrote the lines, no doubt garnered plenty of laughs with them.

Hal Holbrook is the man in the crisp white suit who is getting most of the mileage — and the laughs — out of Twain's sage observations and tall tales these days. But if the 64-year-old actor has clawed his way to the forefront of his profession by mining the legacy of one of America's greatest humorists, it is not merely the richness of the material to which he owes his success. He has learned how to deliver those highly-polished pearls of wisdom, and more importantly, to milk the pauses between them, as shrewdly as any stand-up comic.

Holbrook's study of Twain began in 1947 with a senior-year honors project at Denison University in Granville, Ohio, at the behest of professor Edward Wright. Along with scenes from *As You Like It* and *Hamlet*, Holbrook and his first wife, Ruby, portrayed Elizabeth Barrett and Robert Browning and presented Twain's *An Encounter with an In-*

terviewer — "The one thing you've *got* to do," Wright had urged them. Holbrook told the head of the drama department it was "the corniest thing we've ever read," but did it anyway, with Wright's encouragement.

After a "dreadful" first run-through and a premiere performance of the Twain sketch in the suicide ward of a veteran's hospital — which was only slightly more encouraging — the Holbrooks embarked on a tour of the Southwest with their two-person show. They traveled 40,000 miles in 30 weeks, and gave over 300 performances to elementary, junior and senior high school students. The young couple then graduated to women's clubs and small colleges, where they drew far more appreciative audiences.

By the time the Cleveland-born actor moved to New York in 1952, he and his wife had toured with the show for four years. Offstage, they had also become a threesome, with the recent birth of a daughter. Ruby left the show as a result, and Hal set out on his own.

In desperation, he began to think in terms of a one-man show built around the character of Samuel Clemens and started reading the author's work more seriously, "to take a fresh interest in finding out what made him tick." But he was hesitant at first: "I had been doing Twain in the *Interviewer* sketch for four years but creating him alone on stage was another matter."

However, the young actor wanted to prove to himself that he could do it. He was motivated in part by his drama professor, Ed Wright, who performed a program of comic sketches — and whose sense of timing Holbrook much admired. "I got to studying [his] audiences... and thinking what a joy it would be if I could make people laugh like that," he recalled. He also found acting jobs hard to come by.

Holbrook finally started to put the solo show together early in 1953. Among his most valuable resources was James "Bim" Pond, the son of Twain's lecture manager, whom he had met a few years earlier. Pond approximated Twain's voice for Holbrook, regaled him with anecdotes and provided him with copies of the author's lecture programs, listing the selections Twain had used on *his* tours.

Pond — who represented both Ruth Draper and Cornelia Otis Skinner at the outset of their careers as solo artists — also had a slight influence on the actor's stage characterization. "There was something about him that colored my feelings about Twain," says Holbrook. "Maybe it was his curmudgeon nature."

The eyes of a favorite uncle, and the actor's memory of "the veiled humor that lurked in those eyes," were similarly employed. Holbrook's paternal grandfather, with whom he lived as a boy and greatly admired, was an even stronger inspiration: "My grandfather did not look like Mark Twain, nor did he walk or talk like him, but there was about him a commanding conviction and manly integrity which I feel in the spirit of Mark Twain."

The characterization developed slowly, with each new discovery shifting the weight. Holbrook visited the places where Twain lived to soak up the atmosphere, and examined every photograph he could get his hands on for mannerisms and expressions. The stance, the jut of the head, the solemn countenance, the presence of "a man who is used to center stage" and a hidden sadness were all derived from studying the photographs. The walk he developed intuitively, by shuffling up and down on the deck of a ferryboat.

Hal Holbrook has portrayed Twain at the peak of his "notorious career," as lecturer and raconteur non pareil, for 35 years. The makeup requires four hours.

solemn countenance, the presence of "a man who is used to center stage" and a hidden sadness were all derived from studying the photographs. The walk he developed intuitively, by shuffling up and down on the deck of a ferryboat.

He talked to people who had known Twain, or seen him in action; he read Twain's descriptions of his technique, as well as newspaper reviews of the humorist's platform appearances, which described Twain's surprisingly casual delivery, his "puzzled, careworn expression" and his manner of "[taking] his audience into his confidence with a serious unconventionality..."

The actor realized he had to communicate that eccentricity, "to make Twain seem unconventional to a modern audience." After reading up on the author's smoking habits, he decided on the use of a cigar. Although Twain never smoked on the platform, the gimmick served Holbrook's purpose: to emphasize his uniqueness on the lecture circuit. The smoking of cigars also gave the actor something to do onstage and allowed him to slow the pace of the show, so he could "meander" into a subject.

"Mark Twain had his own way of making a point," Holbrook asserted. "He meandered around it awhile, drawing attention to absurdities like a man sighting along the barrel of a ridiculously warped rifle, but when he pulled the trigger, it generally blew out the bullseye. The meandering gave him time to hone his deadliest weapon — humor. So when the shot came, it had the sweet element of surprise behind it."

Holbrook gave the initial performance of *Mark Twain Tonight!* at the State Teachers College in Lockhaven, Pennsylvania, early in 1954. While "terribly frightened" about his 50-minute solo debut, he was warmly received — although the audience didn't find some of his material as funny as he did.

The actor nearly jettisoned Twain at this point, having just found steady employment in the daytime TV and radio serial, *The Brighter Day*. But he weighed the precarious nature of his profession and realized he could always count on Twain for bookings; he continued working on his own program at night while playing the serial's reformed alcoholic during the day. The soap opera financed the one-man show for the next five years.

The unlikeliest of settings — a tiny nightclub in Greenwich Village — provided Holbrook with invaluable experience in refining his portrayal of the celebrated curmudgeon, and taught him new lessons in audience psychology. Under the most challenging conditions he polished his act nightly at Upstairs at the Duplex, developing a repertoire of two and one-half hours.

The break he hoped for finally came when Ed Sullivan caught his act and asked Holbrook to appear on his television show in 1956. But as his bookings increased and people started to identify him with Twain, he worried that an established star might beat him to Broadway with a one-man show.

He had cause for concern. Veteran character actor Henry Hull (1890–1977), who made a name for himself on Broadway before Holbrook was born, had been playing the humorist on the college and club circuit in his solo *Evening with Mark Twain* for three decades. "Hal may not have been aware of the show, because Henry apparently never performed it in a major venue," observes producer George Spota, who cast Hull as Twain in a projected one-man TV special during the mid-fifties, but was unable to find a sponsor.

Holbrook had more luck. After a 35-minute version of his act at the fabled Lambs Club in New York caught the attention of radio-TV announcer John Lotas, the two of them formed a production company with the intent of getting the show into a Manhattan theatre. After several appearances on Steve Allen's *Tonight* show and a tour of the Midwest, Lotas and co-producer Bunker Jenkins raised the money to open off-Broadway at the Forty-first Street Theatre on April 6, 1959.

Theatre veterans predicted a less-than-favorable reception for the virtually unknown actor. Instead, the 34-year-old Holbrook, made up in white wig and grey mustache as the 70-year-old Twain, played to packed houses and critical acclaim. *Life* magazine called it "the greatest theatrical surprise of the year."

Holbrook was unnerved by the critique of Bim Pond, whose father had represented Twain on the lecture circuit 70 years earlier. On opening night Pond told him, "You're funnier than Mark Twain ever was." Responded Holbrook: "Twain'd climb out of his grave and beat hell out of me if he heard that."

Mark Twain Tonight! garnered an Outer Critics Circle Award and a Vernon Rice Memorial Award by the time the show closed its initial off-Broadway run, after 174 performances. The following year, Holbrook took his show to the Edinburgh Festival and then embarked on a European tour sponsored by the State Department.

The actor had attempted for years "to lose myself in the part — and I mean *lose* myself..." But by this time he had realized that "nobody can be another person. More than that — to do something well, there's got to be something of *you* in it. Now I'm in control," he noted.

Henry Hull toured for decades as Mark Twain, who represented for him "the Spirit of America... growing and vibrant with a golden promise."

When Holbrook as Twain described his boyhood on his uncle's farm, the actor called upon memories of his own youth on *his* uncle's chicken farm. While he found reflections of himself in Twain, and vice versa, there was no identity crisis. Offstage, he was decidedly not Twain, nor did he wish to be: "When the actor who plays Lincoln begins to think he is Lincoln, he is dead."

and TV producers who might employ him; instead, it back-fired — narrow-minded producers offered him "nothing but parts for 70-year-old men."

He fought typecasting by returning to the stage, as Hotspur in *Henry IV, Part I,* at the American Shakespeare Festival in Stratford, Connecticut, and as Lincoln in a revival of *Abe Lincoln in Illinois.* He was then invited to join Manhattan's new Lincoln Center Repertory Company, where he did Arthur Miller's *After the Fall* and *Incident at Vichy.*

Holbrook made a triumphant return to Broadway as Twain in 1966, winning the coveted Tony Award as Best Actor and a Drama Critic's Circle Award for his finely etched portrayal. The role he created for himself was ever more comfortable; even the occasional twitch was more in character than it had been in 1959. "Half my twitches then," he admitted, "were just nerves."

The content of the show was also far more topical, given the climate of the times. While Holbrook changed the material nightly — according his mood and the audience reaction — the structure of the evening was by this time as carefully calibrated as anything Twain ever wrote. "People are bound to come with the creeping feeling that they'll be bored to death. Who wants to see an evening about a literary figure?" he told writer William Goldman.

"My biggest desire was to make them laugh their asses off at the start, so they'd go out at intermission and say, 'This guy's funny.' The second act became the social-comment act. In the last act, I gave them the Twain they'd been expecting all along: warm, whimsical memories of childhood. I think if I'd done the acts the other way around, the third act first, it would have killed it... surprise is the one thing you have going for you. In a one-man show, the little you've got takes on importance. There's drama in a water pitcher if you use it right."

Holbrook eventually cracked "the 70-year-old barrier" that had dogged him for years and went on to play a variety of parts, notably on television as the idealistic Sen. Hayes Stowe in the short-lived series, *The Senator*, Commander Lloyd Bucher in *The Pueblo*, and the title role in *Sandburg's Lincoln* — all three of which won him Emmy Awards. While he has said that he identifies strongly with James Tyrone — the ill-fated protagonist of O'Neill's *Long Day's Journey Into Night*, who was ruined by his success in a single role — the actor has not abandoned the part that made him famous.

At 64, Holbrook does not have to stretch nearly as far in age these days to play Twain. But he takes nothing for granted. He is so precise about the make-up that this task alone requires nearly four hours today. The gait is more casual, the pace more relaxed, the delivery more spontaneous as he chooses from a 12-hour repertoire of material.

Holbrook as Twain absent-mindedly wanders off in the middle of stories, his leg falls asleep — and sometimes even he dozes off. But the humor is sharper and more relevant than ever. "I feel more restful playing him," Holbrook notes, "more free to say things through him about what's going on in the world." To wit: "Washington seems like a stud farm for every jackass in the country."

Holbrook's Twain is in great demand for such topical humor today. Hyperbole aside, however, he has no patent on the part. Any number of hungry young actors have stared enviously at his meal ticket in recent years, and more than a few have been tempted to take a nibble. But such problems come with the territory — Twain himself was plagued by impersonators, and sometimes had to pay their hotel bills when they skipped town. And Twain was Henry Hull's alter ego long before Holbrook adopted the role.

Actor Dean Butler (Almanzo on TV's *Little House on the Prairie*) has contemplated doing a one-man Twain "when Mr. Holbrook is gone." Others have been less patient. In 1968, Holbrook gave John Chappell permission to use excerpts from *Mark Twain Tonight!* in church basements and school auditoriums in a small town in Georgia "on behalf of civil rights." After Chappell created his own show entitled *Mark Twain on Stage* and cost him a booking, Holbrook taped the program, only to discover "he had done a very clever thing. He had taken my show apart, seam by seam, and put it back together in a different format."

In 1973, Michael Randall began offering a show he called *A Dinner Cruise With Mark Twain.* Holbrook called it an infringement of copyright and sued for damages. "Anyone has the right to do Mark Twain... but they have to do the work themselves. Just as I have done the work," says Holbrook. "I have no way of knowing how many actors are stealing my material, but based upon the sleuthing I had to do in the case of two of them, I can guess that a great many actors are stealing it wholesale.

"There are many selections I do which Twain never wrote. I have created them by putting together little pieces of Twain from a variety of sources in his work to create a new selection. I had three of Randall's performances taped and they were replicas of my own material... he had not even bothered to change one word. The judge issued a legal order to Randall never to perform the show again in that manner, never to perform it in a white suit, and not to

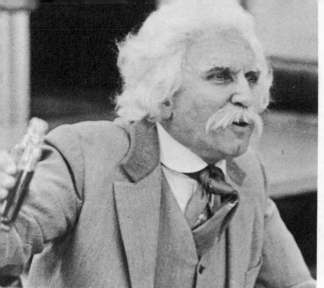

Photo by Fred Watkins

Ray Reinhardt, left, in *An Evening with Mark Twain*; Bill McLinn, right, in *Mark Twain Himself.*

perform it using a cigar on stage — inventions of mine which the judge allowed as being my creation."

Among the many others who portray the famed humorist today — "imposters," as Holbrook once called them — is Bill McLinn, a former Congressional staff member who lectures on social issues, in Twain's words; he has given speeches tailored to college students and corporate executives, as well as church sermons presenting the author's views on disarmament.

McLinn, who began doing Twain as a graduate school project at the University of California at Berkeley in 1975, has performed *Mark Twain Himself* on tour in Europe, Asia and the Soviet Union, where the author of *Tom Sawyer* and *Huckleberry Finn* enjoys huge popularity. He has also run for President as Twain.

"In the realm of theatre, Holbrook is a master," acknowledges McLinn, who admits the actor has cost him a few bookings. "Outside the theatre, I think I have a leg up on him. I'm more flexible, able to do different types of presentations. Twain gave after-dinner speeches, commencement addresses, press conferences and fund-raisers; I do all of that, not just the theatrical performance." He also does question-and-answer sessions, using only Twain's words.

When someone suggested that veteran actor Ray Reinhardt should tour as Twain — after a 20-minute presentation in the role — he argued against it: "I said, 'Oh, no, Hal Holbrook is definitive in the part.' They said, 'Yeah, but he doesn't go to the smaller places."

Reinhardt, a founding member of San Francisco's American Conservatory Theatre — where he played Stanley Kowalski in *A Streetcar Named Desire* and the title role in *Cyrano de Bergerac* — has been performing *An Evening With Mark Twain* at colleges and men's clubs since 1985.

While he concedes that the show is "not too much different" from Holbrook's, Reinhardt says his presentation is "a little more serious. I don't use as much humor." The program is also different in shape and content; it is primarily about life on the Mississippi.

"I don't think of myself as competing with Holbrook," states Reinhardt. "*I'm* different — the way it's going to come across is different. It's like any other role made famous by another actor, like Hamlet or Kowalski. At first you say to yourself, 'What the hell am I doing?' You're intimidated by Brando. But then I found another way of doing it, a way of being myself."

48th St. Theatre

PLAYBILL

a weekly magazine for theatregoers

SHAKESPEARE'S
"AGES OF MAN"

Homage to the Bard

Eighteenth century Irish actor Charles Macklin was renowned for his interpretation of Shylock, but his less than scholarly lectures on Shakespeare were the object of ridicule. Macklin, who was said to have invented the art of teaching acting, disobeyed the first rule of public oratory — he was woefully ignorant in the subject matter.

John Gielgud and Ian McKellen, whose well-traveled solo recitals have venerated each of them as the preeminent Shakespearean actor of his generation, both downplayed the scholarship inherent in their programs. Gielgud, who toured with *Ages of Man* for a decade, has long had a tendency toward self-deprecation. "The joke is that people think of me as an intellectual actor," he noted in one of his memoirs. "Yet I have always trusted almost entirely to observation, emotion and instinct."

McKellen, who once aspired to be a teacher, is quick to dismiss the lecture aspect of *Ian McKellen Acting Shakespeare*. "The atmosphere I'm trying to create is that of a party, in which I'm the host and the audience arrives to meet the guest of honor, who is William Shakespeare," he told an interviewer. "I'm not trying to tell anybody anything — not trying to teach anything. Heaven forbid! I'm trying to move Shakespeare from the classroom... and put him where he belongs, and that is the theatre."

Both actors parlayed their adoration for the Bard and their knowledge of the theatre into hugely successful one-man shows. But Gielgud's and McKellen's respective entertainments were far more than showcases for their mercurial acting talents; they paid homage to Shakespeare by communicating their excitement and enthusiasm for his vast riches, bringing him to vibrant life for many who were relatively unfamiliar with his work.

John Gielgud was born with the theatre — and the Bard — in his blood. His maternal grandmother Kate Terry, her daughters Ellen and Marion, and his paternal great grandmother Aniela Aszpergerowa were all illustrious actresses known for their Shakespearean roles. Young John was a stagestruck schoolboy when he first played Shylock and Mark Anthony; at 17, he made his debut at the Old Vic — in an unbilled walk-on — as the Herald in *Henry V*.

As the 25-year-old star of the Vic Company in 1929, his Romeo "gave little hint of the power to come, although he spoke beautifully," according to director Harcourt Williams. That same season, he essayed Richard II, Macbeth and Hamlet with great success. When he reprised the latter role at Elsinore a decade later, Copenhagen newspaper headlines called him "The World's Best Hamlet."

Gielgud, whose reputation for irreverent humor is second only to his renown as an actor, once suggested to Emlyn Williams a production of *A Midsummer Night's Dream* in the nude — retitled *Bottom*. Williams was "a youthful fifty" and one year Gielgud's junior when he proposed, on a somewhat more serious note, that his lifelong friend attempt a one-man Shakespeare anthology along the lines of Williams' *Charles Dickens*. But the actor protested: "Oh no, I think one should keep that sort of thing for one's old age."

Yet Gielgud felt older than his half century. Out of touch and "old hat" by his own admission, he was unable to relate to the writers of his time; he longed to do something avant-garde, something more modern than Ibsen or Chekhov, but rejected plays like Samuel Beckett's *Endgame*. By then he had also been dethroned by Laurence Olivier as England's most popular classical actor.

When the British Arts Council asked him to do an evening of poetry "as a kind of compliment" in 1956, Gielgud offered them a Shakespeare program. He then asked the advice of George Rylands, the noted academic who had directed his 1944 *Hamlet*. Rylands suggested his anthology, *The Ages of Man*, as a basis; the actor agreed and hired a lutanist to round out the presentation. *The Times* of London called it "a desecration of Shakespeare."

Such harsh words were foreign to Gielgud. By this point in his career, he had appeared in over 40 stage productions of the Bard's plays, and directed nearly 20 of them; reviewers were seldom less than generous in their praise. Undaunted by the critique, Gielgud altered the structure of the anthology and dispensed with the lutanist. In September 1957, after playing Prospero at Stratford, he gave the first public performance of his one-man show at the Edinburgh Festival.

The presentation began rather tentatively, on an unusually warm afternoon, with a tuxedo-clad Gielgud "reading noble verse in an equally noble voice," recalled *Sunday Times* critic Harold Hobson. "Then Sir John sprang back from his reading desk, broke his reliance on the text, and shocked our drowsiness into intent awareness with an extremely vigorous rendering of [Mercutio's] Queen Mab speech... it set the audience cheering," noted Hobson. "Above all, in the musical despair of *Richard II*, in his luxurious savouring of the perverse pleasures of humiliation

John Gielgud as Cassius in MGM's *Julius Caesar* — a role he first essayed at Stratford in 1950 and reprised, sans costume, in his one-man show.

and defeat... we had the awe and majesty of an excited intellect, of a superb presence, of an incomparable voice."

Following Gielgud's triumph at Edinburgh, producer Jerry Leider arranged a tour of Europe and the United States. The actor was skeptical of his reception in America. Although he had toured with *Hamlet* and made other appearances on Broadway, he questioned his reputation; he had been seen in few films at this stage and felt he was past his prime. Yet he was encouraged by a distant recollection of his great aunt, Ellen Terry, who had toured America and Australia with "some sort of lecture" on Shakespeare's heroines.

Terry — famed for her portrayal of Portia — "seemed to be able to relive her youthful parts," recalled her grand nephew, "and I felt here was an opportunity to show myself to the present generation in parts in which I'd been a success, things I'd played and loved when I was young."

Nevertheless, Gielgud was an unlikely candidate for solo theatre. He had always been less concerned with his own performance than the overall success of the production in which he was appearing. Unlike the famous British actor-managers of the past who surrounded themselves with second-rate talent, he had never turned the spotlight on himself; he focused on the ensemble, and worked whenever possible with actors he admired and respected.

Performers like Peggy Ashcroft, who played Ophelia to his Hamlet, were invaluable in more ways than one — as Emlyn Williams inadvertently reminded him when they met in New York. "I was rather embarrassed as to whether he would resent my success in a field in which he was already an acknowledged master," Gielgud noted recently. "So I said, 'Didn't you dread the fire engines and ambulances shrieking by, and knowing they would be sure to pass the theatre during one's quietest passages?' To which Emlyn replied with a knowing smile: 'Yes, and you can't hurry up your timing so that they would go by when Peggy is speaking!'"

Thus limited, Gielgud would stand behind a lectern, a leather-bound script his only prop, and begin with Jacques' "seven ages" speech from *As You Like It.* He would then proceed to people the bare stage with an army of eloquent soldiers: the insipid young Romeo, the cynical Cassius, the disenchanted Henry VI, the earthbound Caliban, the woman-hating Benedick, the soul-searching Hamlet, an indignant Hotspur defending himself against insubordination, the broken Lear grieving for the dead Cordelia.

Though his three-act adaptation of Rylands' cradle-to-grave anthology displayed the breadth and humanity of his favorite playwright, Gielgud conceded that the show "was a bit snobbish because in it I play nothing but patricians and kings and heroes." The coarse-bred personalities of Malvolio and Iago, he felt, were clearly beyond his range: "I think it's just something I can't do, and it isn't that I think I'm grand or aristocratic, but I know that I make that effect upon an audience, whether it's true or not."

Gielgud was comfortable with his limitations — as he saw them — but disheartened by those of theatregoers. "Audiences are not prepared to sit through a long — not dull — but rather measured passage in Shakespeare, so that they will come to the exciting bit. They want to get on from the 'To be or not to be' to 'What a rogue and peasant slave' in two easy lessons because they know those bits, and anything that isn't famous is apt to be ignored," he lamented to an interviewer. "I feed them too many purple passages. Therefore you have got, as a director, to make it more and more and more exciting, otherwise they won't listen to it."

The recital not only illustrated Gielgud's "appetite for risks" but accomplished "something else of great importance: it [deflated] the myth that Gielgud is simply a superb musical instrument... He doesn't simply speak verse, he *acts* it," observed critic Michael Billington.

Kenneth Tynan lauded the "thrilling instrument that commands the full tonal range of both viola and cello," but criticized Gielgud for his lack of movement, labeling him "the finest actor on earth from the neck up." In his defense, Gielgud asserted that his objective was "to indicate the character with the voice, depending on the part. I always try to avoid too much gesture... the tendency in doing Shakespeare has too often been to substitute activity and restlessness for the musical and athletic power of the verse," he said. He would later recall the solo show as "one of the hardest things I ever tackled."

Gielgud — who had lent his talents in the preceding years to such non-Shakespearean roles as Sir Joseph Surface in *The School for Scandal* and John Worthing in *The Importance of Being Earnest* — recharged his batteries with the success of *Ages of Man*, touring Canada, Scandinavia, Israel and Russia before he set it down in 1967. After proving himself in such contemporary plays as David Storey's *Home* and Harold Pinter's *No Man's Land*, he returned to Shakespeare in the seventies, reprising Prospero and Caesar at the National Theatre. He even played the Bard himself, as an embittered old man, in Edward Bond's parable, *Bingo*.

Ian McKellen — whom Laurence Olivier once called

"the greatest young actor in the English language" — like Gielgud played his first Shakespearean roles while still in school. At Cambridge, with the encouragement of don George Rylands, McKellen became president of the Marlowe Society and in his first year played a much-acclaimed Justice Swallow in *Henry IV*, *Part 2*.

After making his London debut in 1964, McKellen joined Olivier's National Theatre Company. He essayed a great variety of roles both modern and classical before his triumphant reign at the 1969 Edinburgh Festival, as Shakespeare's *Richard II* and Marlowe's *Edward II*. The 30-year-old McKellen then toured Britain in both roles and played to sell-out crowds in London.

In 1974, he joined the Royal Shakespeare Company in 1974, giving memorable performances in Stratford and London as Leontes in *The Winter's Tale* and Sir Toby Belch. The highlight of his four seasons with RSC was a bold, unconventional Macbeth who made audience members accomplices to his crimes, creating what one critic termed "a stifling intimacy" in a studio production.

While at Stratford McKellen was invited to do something for the 1976 Edinburgh Festival. He mulled it over and finally agreed to put together "something about Shakespeare." The result was a solo piece that conveyed his enthusiasm for the Bard and underscored his vision of the playwright as a man of the theatre whose concern for that world was "metaphysical and all-embracing." The show derived its title from "a pun that nobody gets but me," McKellen asserts.

"It's called *Acting Shakespeare*, which is indeed an actor acting Shakespeare, but it also means an actor talking not about the philosopher Shakespeare or the poet Shakespeare, but the *acting* Shakespeare, the Shakespeare who was an actor and interested in acting." The show — which critic Stephen Farber called "a distinctive theatrical experiment: part autobiography, part classroom lecture, part vaudeville show" — consists of anecdotes about the playwright and productions of his work, analyses of his verse, reminiscences about McKellen's acting career, imitations of other actors and passages from the plays.

McKellen developed and refined the program over a long period of time, performing it "off and on — very much more off than on," most frequently as a benefit. In 1979 he embarked on a British Council-sponsored tour with the show, which took him to Israel and Scandinavia. The following year he brought the program to the U.S., after signing to play Antonio Salieri in *Amadeus* by Peter Shaffer.

"*Amadeus* is a play where the character spends a great deal of time talking to the audience," he later observed. "That was something I'd never done before and I thought the Shakespeare show would be a good way to practice getting the audience on my side, which I felt Salieri had to do." His bravura portrayal of Mozart's envious rival garnered a flock of awards, including the Tony.

McKellen began to look upon his solo performance — which he once described as "midway between a chat show and classical acting" — as "a visa" to different parts of the world, in between other roles. "I certainly don't want to become one of those actors who are known for their one-man shows," he told an interviewer.

He didn't explore the show's commercial possibilities until he brought *Acting Shakespeare* back to North America for an extended run in 1983-84. McKellen found himself playing to packed houses and taking curtain calls to wildly

Ian McKellen, who finds the Bard "profoundly relevant to the current political scene," has toured the world in *Acting Shakespeare*.

enthusiastic reception, particularly in his Broadway run at the 999-seat Ritz Theatre.

Like its precursor, *Ages of Man*, McKellen's program begins with *As You Like It* and concludes with *The Tempest*. Yet he was not intimidated at the prospect of being compared to Gielgud when he started out. "I was never worried because I came on with an enthusiasm that is entirely genuine. I knew it was going to be all right. I had something I wanted to say," asserts McKellen.

"I wanted the play to reflect my own feelings about Shakespeare, what it was about him that makes me respond to him so personally, and so I knew I didn't want to come out in a tuxedo and perform speeches. I also wanted the show to be entertaining and contemporary, because I think the theatre is about *today*. It has to do with telling us how life might be better, how our appreciation of life might be deepened. And so I thought, 'I'll just put on an ordinary shirt and trousers and walk out on to the stage, start talking and see what happens.'"

McKellen's phrase-by-phrase, line-by-line analysis of Macbeth's "Tomorrow and tomorrow and tomorrow" soliloquy is, for many, the high point of the evening. Frederick Guidry of *The Christian Science Monitor* felt the show reached its climax with McKellen's performance of a lengthy scene from *Macbeth*, and marveled at its intensity. "Words and theories about acting seemed to fade in the presence of such a demonstration of it," he noted.

At least one critic was appalled by the very same demonstration. Jonathan Saville of the San Diego, Calif. *Reader* was impressed by the actor's scholarship and his rapport with the audience, and amused by the parodies of "bad" Shakespearean acting — including a "tremble-perfect" imitation of Gielgud's Lear. But he concluded that McKellen's own acting "is so bad that one can scarcely believe it is intended as an illustration of how Shakespeare ought to be acted." Saville advised aspiring Shakespearean actors: "Do what Ian McKellen says, don't do what he does."

The British have no monopoly on one-man shows that pay tribute to the Bard, as two young American actors are currently demonstrating. Neither Benjamin Stewart nor Fred Curchack have McKellen's credentials; both, however, share his affection for Shakespeare's language and his love of theatre.

Stewart, a Houston-born aficionado of literature, was working as a radio announcer in 1969 when an amateur group decided to stage Shakespeare's *Venus and Adonis* and asked him to do the narration. After moving to Los Angeles to pursue an acting career, he tried to interest producers in his own adaptation of the epic love poem. "Nobody took me up on it," he explains, "so I decided to design it as a solo performance."

While Stewart was preparing his dramatization, Irene Worth staged a one-woman version at the Stratford, Ontario, Shakespeare Festival. "I tend not to agree with her interpretation. I think the poem is a man's piece," states the actor, who performs in a dark sweat shirt and sweat pants on an empty stage. "It's not my sole property," he concedes. "But nobody is quite as attached to it as I am."

The burly performer is the first to admit that he is unlikely casting for either the goddess of love or the supple young object of her infatuation. "I do not try to become Venus or Adonis," he told an interviewer. "I try to become the poem." Stewart's "manifestation" of the piece, which debuted in Los Angeles in 1984, has been staged at a

Benjamin Stewart in his rendition of *Venus and Adonis*.

number of Shakespeare festivals.

Unlike Worth, who did an edited version, Stewart presents the 1,194-line work in its entirety, with all of the poem's integrity and erotic humor intact. The actor, a long-time member of the Arizona Theatre Company in Tucson, refuses to cut a

word of the text, which he describes as "one hour and 10 minutes of non-stop fever-pitch iambic pentameter."

Fred Curchack has no such allegiance for the classics he adapts to the stage. But what the New York native and High School of Performing Arts graduate lacks in reverence for the Bard, he makes up in imagination and resourcefulness. His one-man, five-character version of *The Tempest* strips Shakespeare's last play to the bare essentials — then employs poor-theatre techniques and junkyard props to conjure up a spectacular show of illusions.

"I'm not trying to glorify poverty, but I think it's very important to find sources of inspiration that don't rely on money — both in the theatre and in life," says the prolific actor-director, who estimates that the show cost less than $100 to put together. Unlike McKellen, who "never liked one-man shows," Curchack has a decided preference for such "financially pragmatic" productions; he has created

seven of them to date. "You don't have to wait for an entire cast to catch up with you," he reasons.

Curchack's *Stuff as Dreams Are Made On* is less an adaptation of *The Tempest* than a satire on the futility of trying to perform it as a 75-minute solo piece — in which he has cast himself as a bumbling, burned-out actor. The energetic performer portrays Prospero, Ariel and Caliban with masks, and supplies a falsetto voice for the doll that represents Miranda. He blends Balinese and South Indian dance movements with Japanese Noh Theatre techniques, using shadow puppets, flashlights and cigarette lighters to provide the special effects.

Curchack, who teaches at the University of Texas at Dallas and is often invited to international theatre festivals, lets the audience "more or less play the enemy" as a means of "getting people involved." He also improvises freely on Shakespeare's text — purists be damned — in a further effort to break down the invisible fourth wall that separates performer from audience. Latecomers are asked to account for their tardiness, then told: "It's okay. The play is about forgiveness, so I'll forgive you — and when I'm done, you can forgive me."

The question is, would Shakespeare forgive him? "I think he'd love it," says Curchack. "On one level, he asks the clowns not to overdo it. But I think he'd find some aspects of the show profoundly truthful to the core of his intent. *The Tempest* is not just a farewell to theatre — it's an existential map of a very high order, and I deal with it on that plane."

Opposite: Fred Curchack heads the one-man cast of *Stuff as Dreams are Made On*.

SHOWBILL

PROVINCETOWN PLAYHOUSE

PAT CARROLL in

GERTRUDE STEIN
GERTRUDE STEIN
GERTRUDE STEIN

Monologue: Pat Carroll

"Didn't she used to be a comedian, that Pat Carroll? Well, I didn't think this was very funny." A great roar of laughter tumbles forth from Pat Carroll herself, provoked by her remembrance of a middle-aged, Midwestern fan who evidently didn't know what to expect from Carroll's one-woman show on Gertrude Stein.

But even the actress — a seasoned veteran of TV situation comedies, quiz shows, and dinner-theater — concedes she was an unlikely candidate to portray the expatriate writer who collected art and artists with equal passion. "It wouldn't have happened unless I'd cast myself," she said in a recent interview. "I wasn't sure at all, but I was willing to take a gamble."

It was by far the biggest gamble of her career, which began in summer stock in 1947. When Carroll found herself flat on her back early in 1976, recuperating from knee surgery, she realized few producers were looking for "aging, overweight actresses with limps." After examining her dim career prospects — and seeing William Windom's one-man Thurber — she became "morbidly obsessed" with creating her own solo theatrical project.

The Louisiana native had put together an autobiographical revue two years earlier, but An Evening With — Who? *had no life beyond dinner-theater. A planned evening of women's poetry and mime was no longer feasible, due to the knee surgery; a salute to solo performers Ruth Draper, Cornelia Otis Skinner and Angna Enters was contemplated, but also dropped.*

As she racked her brain for inspiration, the personality who came most frequently to mind was Gertrude Stein. The subject was just as frequently dismissed. Carroll had never been enamored of her work. "I found her repetitious form childish, her mind jumps quixotic and her general mode irritating and confusing," she admits. "I felt she was a hoax."

When the idea continued to gnaw away at her, Carroll read everything written by and about the influential and controversial Stein, whose "insatiable appetite for people" turned her Paris salon into a gathering place for the likes of Picasso, Hemingway, Joyce, Fitzgerald, Matisse and Cézanne. "I discovered it was not Miss Stein's work I wanted to do, it was her life," Carroll told an interviewer. "What I looked for was her humor, and I found it... Then I became hooked not only on the colors of her life, but the lives that intertwined with and crossed hers."

As Carroll assimilated those colors, young Texas playwright Marty Martin wove his passion for Stein into a impressionistic fabric of monologue that had all of Stein's vibrant personality and peculiar writing style, and none of her words. Martin also came up with an ingenious premise — he set the play on the night before Stein and Alice B. Toklas were to be evicted from their cluttered apartment at 27 rue de Fleurus.

"That had every reason in the world for this spewing out," affirms Carroll. *"I think it was a psychologist who said that moving, next to death, was probably the most traumatic experience you ever go through. I vouch for that. I just translated my knowledge of what it feels like to move, to that moment. It left Stein vulnerable, open, exasperated, frightened — certainly remembering."*

Gertrude Stein Gertrude Stein Gertrude Stein *opened at*

the Circle Repertory Theatre in New York on June 6, 1979, and later transferred to the Provincetown Playhouse before touring the United States. Carroll's portrayal of Stein — a characterization modeled on her producer's mother — brought her a Drama Desk Award, an Outer Critics Circle Award and a Best Actress citation from the New York Drama Critics.

"It's ironic that this old baggy-pants actress ends up doing classic theatre," says Carroll, who recently played the Nurse in Romeo and Juliet *and now aspires to do* Mother Courage *and* Trojan Women. *She does not look back with disdain on her early years as a TV comedienne and game show panelist, however.* "I am grateful for television," *notes the entertainer, who won an Emmy in 1956 for her role on* Caesar's Hour *and was subsequently featured on* The Danny Thomas Show. *"I play the same theatres I played as a very young actress at a much higher price, and I probably wouldn't be playing there had it not been for television. I do not bite the good hand that has fed me."*

Carroll is currently working on two solo programs, including a four-character piece entitled Merry Wives and Widows, *and a secret project she will not discuss. At one point, she considered doing a show on anthropologist Margaret Mead, but abandoned the idea after a year's research when she realized Mead lacked a sense of humor.*

Among a myriad of other projects, Carroll has given thought to writing a book entitled Wrestling and Gertrude Stein. *"When we arrived at the convention center in Myrtle Beach, South Carolina,"* she explains, *"on the marquee it said, 'Wrestling and Gertrude Stein,' and I didn't know which I was. Or was I to do both?!"* The recollection prompts another burst of hearty laughter.

If I ever meet Gertrude Stein in Heaven, she would either like me and I would like her, or we would hate each other — immediately. But I have a feeling I would like her. Every book that's been written about Paris in the 1920s, by people who lived at that time, all had something to say about Gertrude. She was never bland. This was a personality who either rubbed you the wrong way or lighted up your life. How many theatrical characters are like that?

If she hadn't had a sense of humor, I don't think I could have played her. The humor is in the books. I laughed out loud a couple of times in *Everybody's Autobiography*, and *The Autobiography of Alice B. Toklas*. What a hoot. The woman had a tremendous sense of her own importance, but she occasionally would throw that to the winds and be real honest, which I adore. Those were the qualities that fascinated me with Stein.

I don't know how you could do a show on someone you didn't admire, unless there was a dramatic excitement about the character. About the literary works I'm not a scholar, but as far as Stein's life is concerned, I think she's one of the most brilliant pieces of work that's ever been made. From the moment I got that sweep, I thought, "Wow! What a role." And it wasn't even written yet. But the *life* was there.

When I started out to do the show, I was really in a rotten state. My personal life was lousy; my professional life was even worse. But sometimes when you're at the bottom, and you must get something going, it's the greatest time in your life — you know why you want to do it, but you don't know how you're going to do it. You just keep going, straight ahead 'til morning... sometimes even without faith, you keep going.

Success and failure have nothing to do with it, because you learn more about yourself as a human being during that process of going straight ahead. I was more proud of myself for having completed something than I was about the show. With my Irish proclivity for having eight projects going at once and maybe not any of them will I see to fulfillment, I finally went, "I can't die..." I *know* that I have that propensity. Success or not, I can see it through to the bitter end. The most exciting thing about living is finding out you're capable of something — that you're not deterred.

I could not have done Stein 20 years ago. I didn't have the experience, I didn't have the freedom as a performer... I wasn't ready for it on any level — emotionally, mentally, or theatrically. I built a role for myself at exactly the right time. Everything I've ever done is in there. Broadway, television, radio, commercials, nightclubs... It has aspects of vaudeville in it. It's everything. I always played it like it was a play. And a symphony.

It was a wonderful piece by the writer, into which I fed with great joy. Marty Martin wrote it, but I know what I put into it, because it was like a dress to be tailor-made for me. I didn't commission this to have somebody else do it.

There's not an actual quote from Stein in the entire play; it's all paraphrased. It's like a spoof, a sendup. Even the so-called scholars... I laugh at scholars sometimes because

Pat Carroll's evocation of Gertrude Stein excavated the writer's complex personality from "an academic and literary cloud."

Photo by Gerry Goodstein

they're so smitten with their own world, they can't see the reality, that the emperor is naked. There is not a single quote, and the estate could never take us to task for anything. Marty I think was terribly clever for doing that. It's a strange thing; his rhythms are Steinien. It's like a good drummer hears a beat...Marty heard that beat and copied it.

When Marty sent me the first act, I flipped. It was absolutely on the button. The second act had to be rewritten twice, because he continued in the same vein. I knew that could not happen; *I* wouldn't come back to the theatre. If the first act didn't hook me and the second act didn't get me farther along, I'd get up and leave. I said, "Something marvelous has to happen in that second act, Marty... it has to have conflict, and it has to resolve like a regular play does. I don't want to play an entire two hours of anecdotes. There's no emotional involvement."

If we believe in that marvelous thing that happens between live human beings, whether it's in a church or a theatre or a concert hall... something electric happens. I'm not talking about the bravos and the standing up at the end, there's something that happens in the middle and it is electrical; we transmit something to each other.

Otherwise there's somebody up there posturing and blowing off steam. So what? If we can't transmit passion, and we can't transmit deep concern, deep joy, deep elation, deep hatred, what the hell are we doing? And I've done all the junk in the world, so I know that you can transmit something more important than the junk. But that's the actor's gift, nothing to do with the writing.

When I started working on the play, I went and got as many recordings as I could, of both Ruth Draper and Cornelia Otis Skinner. It's what I call the old-fashioned monologue — directing the conversation to people who are supposedly there. I'm uncomfortable with that. I suppose if I were forced to do it, I could. But there *is* an audience there; who are we kidding?

The first day I started working with the director, Milton Moss, he said, "Why are you talking to the audience?" I said, "Because they're here. Maybe I've invited them here, I don't know. I have nobody else to talk to." He said, "How did they get here?" I said, "How do I know? They're here; let them listen to me. I love an audience." I had to talk to them. I knew that, from the moment I first read the play; I *have* to communicate to the audience.

I had never worked with Milton before; we got along famously. The first day he said, "I hate Gertrude Stein." I said, "I'm not too fond of her either, but let's go to work."

He asked me to arrive with the words learned, a very wise move on his part. I'd never done that before. I arrived with the first act and part of the second act learned — so we could deal immediately with these other issues, like who are you talking to? You can't deal with that issue if you're looking at the script and bumping around.

A lot of times he would just listen to me. He'd say, "You don't believe a word you're saying. What are you talking about?" It surprised me how much I knew about Stein. I had to be devil's advocate when he was asking me questions. He'd say, "Okay, you know that, now let the audience know."

Milton said, "Look, in order to take the onus off this thing, why don't we get another story line. There was this little Jewish girl in Philadelphia who went to Europe..." The analogy was wonderful. It took for us all the heavy "we're dealing with a legend" sort of thing off, and we could joke and make light of it... it made the whole process much easier.

This was a human being who lived, who had aspirations, who had problems like everybody else. It may interest you, it may not... but this person shared this planet at a different place in time. Look what they did, look at the way they thought about life.

When you go to a cocktail party or a small dinner party, you meet new people. And you hear stories of their lives. I thought, treat this show like a cocktail party. Don't make it like it has important quotes but, these are my friends... I'm sorry you don't know them, but I think you'd love them.

Some people felt I was snobbish in playing Stein, a little pompous at times. But I never felt about Stein any other way than, I am so excited as an actress to introduce you to one of the most intriguing persons — whether you like it or not is okay by me. As a hostess in my home, I try to mix people — you know you've given a good party if nobody wants to leave. *That* is a great party. It's not the food, it's not the booze, it's the people.

I thought, how could anybody not be interested in these *people* — a cross section of some of the world's great writers, artists and eccentrics? Some people were not interested. You cannot communicate all the time. I always thought of this play as being a buffet — some days the herring went well, some days the potato salad went, some times the roast beef went, other times the cheese. It was not up to me to tell you [the audience] what you wanted; it was up to you to decide on my delightful little buffet, what you wanted to take.

When I felt that way about my own giggling excitement — when I approached it as being a hostess — the show always seemed to sparkle. If at other times I became pedantic — "Oh, you're going to love it because it's very interesting" — it [died]. The minute I kept that sense of "Oh, God, I can't wait to introduce you to these people," it always worked.

I think people who actually knew Stein found my portrayal of her a bit softer that she actually was, less angular, not in physicality but in personality. Anita Loos took me to task and said, "Oh, my dear, Stein was a bitch." I said, "Would you have wanted to sit here for two hours and see the story of a bitch?" She said, "No, I guess you're doing the Stein she would have wanted."

And why not? That's what the theatre's about. Many of the kings of England weren't exactly the way Shakespeare portrayed them, either. So it finally is in the theatre to take that, without being libelous or creating untruth about the person's life... I think the magic is putting in those colors, according to your own creative feelings about the person.

I don't know, maybe I copped out, maybe I didn't make her as assertive as she was. That's a possibility. The director used to keep saying to me, "Let the warts show. Don't try like every actress to be loved." He was absolutely right. The times I wanted to be loved, it never worked. When I just wanted it to be what was there, it always worked, because her humanity came through; her warts showed. We all have warts; we may put makeup on them, but we all have them.

Gertrude Stein is a public figure anybody can do. There is a woman in San Francisco who is doing a one-woman Stein; it is a totally lesbian approach, which does not interest me at all. Marty asked me, "How do you want to deal with Stein's homosexuality?" I said, "Honestly. You're not going to throw that out or you lose the texture of the life… but I don't want a lesbian play. It's got to be in there, but it's got to be subtext."

I said, "Marty, nobody is going to sit in the theatre for a page and a half of her mewings about her first homosexual affair. You're going to offend the gay people and you're going to offend the straights. Do that in a minute in a half." He said, "I can't do that." I said, "Yes, you can." I think it's one of the best moments in the play. It always works, for those people who want to accept what it says; for those who don't… it goes right over their heads. And to play it was extraordinary. Because I knew… I would sense from the audience who was accepting it and who was letting it go and who was rejecting it… wonderful. It was so exciting — I couldn't wait for that moment in the play.

Where it came to the fight with her brother, Leo Stein, I said, "Now *there* is something that's going to hit everyone, because everybody has had a split in their life, brothers and sisters, husbands and wives, lovers, parents and children."

There comes that point of separation, growing apart. I said, "There will be such identification with everyone, man and woman, in the audience." I cannot tell you, the number of people who came backstage and said, "Oh, my god, I had a fight like that with my father... my husband... my brother..." I was right. You have to know: *that* will strike a cord in people.

I fought the director about the segment on her writing style. I said, "Come on, who's going to be interested?" He said, "It was *very* important to her." I said, "It's not working for me." He said, "I don't care; you've got to keep it in..." I got a knot in my belly, I was so upset by that segment. The number of painters, writers, actors who reacted — creative people react because everybody's had that clogged pipe. I said to the director, "I was wrong... I did not sense it." It may not mean anything to Joe and Mary Smith, but they're going to be affected by something else.

I don't how people who do one-person shows can do it without that close work with the director. I don't know how it's done any other way. But my experience is empirical. There's no theory, there's no book. Everybody who does this calls everybody else for information. The uses of one-person theatre are so unique that it is really based on the project, the actor or actress who does it, and at what point they start. We can encourage each other...

You have to do it by trial and error; each show is totally unique. Julie Harris' success has been predicated mostly I think on her reputation with audiences. This doesn't take one iota away from her performance — it means people were willing to see her do Emily Dickinson or whoever because they love Julie Harris. And rightly so. She and James Whitmore could be one-person repertory theatres.

My bonnet is off to anybody who takes this risk. None of these people — with the exception of Hal Holbrook — ever stood in a saloon, did a solo performance to that extent. It takes a lot to stand up there by yourself, and expect to hold an audience. It's an act of courage for any actor to step on the stage, and then to do it *by yourself?* When they can throw things and there's only one person there — that is very courageous.

Now everybody wants to do it because it seems economically feasible, and we all have those little annuities in our back pocket — but you have to respect it. You have to give as much effort, as much worry, as much time and consideration as if you were doing a musical. I was most fortunate in getting Mary Ellyn Devery's services as a producer because she took that burden off my head. Up to that point I'd been producing. You just can't do it all; it's almost impossible.

At one point I went to a hypnotist because it was the first time I'd done two hours alone on the stage. It's been abused in the press — people say, "she was hypnotized to talk for two hours." Wrong. I had 35 years experience making a living talking, before I went to him. But I was fearful of retention. I said, "My fear is, I'm going to go up [blank]." We started talking and I heard myself say, "I'm afraid of being boring." I said, "Wait a minute, I think that's the reason I'm here."

I started telling him about the show. The hypnotist said, "You are not boring. If I were directing this, I'd tell you to play it exactly the way you're doing it now, because your eyes are light. Your body is so filled with enthusiasm and energy... If your play is really like that, you're never going to bore people."

I took three sessions with him, and I came to the conclusion that I was going to go up, which I did. I had one experience, after 200 performances in New York. I was doing a matinee... in the middle of the first act, I didn't know where I was... I looked out; I thought, "What are you people doing here?" I looked at my hands; they were dripping with perspiration. I thought, I'd better leave the stage — but if I leave, I'll never come back. I thought, wait a minute, what did the doctor say? Relax... breathe deeply... I suddenly got it back.

My dresser met me when I came offstage. I said, "I don't know the second act..." I burst into tears; I went down to my dressing room. Mary, my producer, came in. She said, "Well, what have we here? We have an actress who's done 200 performances of this show, and you can't remember the second act?" She said, "That's all right, don't be upset. I'll go out and make an announcement to the audience that you've been taken ill, and their money will be refunded at the box office — and you're going to pay for it." I said, "WAIT A MINUTE. I THINK I REMEMBER."

I couldn't remember the second act, but I thought, "I'm not going to return the money." Good old pragmatic actress. I went upstairs and started the second act... by the end of the first two speeches I was fine. What had happened was I'd forgotten to eat breakfast and I had a sugar drop. I never did that again.

I put the show to bed at the end of the fifth year. At the start I said a prayer: "Good lord, I need this. If it's to be wonderful, give me five years." I had five years, almost to the day.

I always said I would never do Stein if I got bored, if I was doing it just for the money. It wasn't totally a labor of love — I didn't do it for the adoration of Gertrude Stein. I'm a professional actress; I make my living doing this. But I was beginning to get mind-weary. There were certain parts of the play I was nodding through. No way you can do that, because the audience is the other actor, and if that ball isn't bounced constantly... they are being cheated. I said, this is the end of it.

How any critic assessed the play or me as the actress never bothered me. My most important critique comes from the audience. I communicate to you, is it returned, do we have that thing going between us, are we playing the game? As an actress I'm not playing for eternity; that's not my business. It's a fast ball game, and sometimes called for rain or darkness... you've got to do it now, now is the important thing.

GROVE THEATRE

SHORE ROAD BELFAST 15 phone 76463

COMMENCING MONDAY, 25TH OCTOBER, 1965

BRENDAN SMITH in association with EDWARDS-MacLIAMMOIR

DUBLIN GATE THEATRE PRODUCTIONS LTD.

and the ARTS COUNCIL OF NORTHERN IRELAND

presents

MICHEAL
MacLIAMMOIR

in

**TALKING
ABOUT
YEATS**

on

MONDAY

TUESDAY

WEDNESDAY

at 8 p.m.

**I MUST
BE
TALKING
TO MY
FRIENDS**

on

THURSDAY

FRIDAY

SATURDAY

at 8 p.m.

directed by HILTON EDWARDS

Compiled and written by MICHEAL MacLIAMMOIR

The Irish Tradition

"It's been said that inside every fat man is a skinny man trying to get out. Inside every Irishman is a one-man show trying to get out," asserts Shay Duffin, the Dublin-born actor best known for his solo portrayal of Brendan Behan. Inasmuch as Ireland has given the world more literary giants than perhaps any other country, it is hardly surprising that the Irish have been responsible for so many solo entertainments.

The works of Samuel Beckett alone have supplied the creative backbone of at least seven one-person shows to date. Oscar Wilde, George Bernard Shaw, James Joyce and Brendan Behan have inspired four or more programs each; William Butler Yeats, John Millington Synge, Jonathan Swift and others have also unwittingly lent their talents to this unique form of theatre.

Cultural heritage is a prominent factor in the Celtic propensity toward theatre of the individual. Long before radio and television reached out to the remotest crags and crannies of Ireland, there was the *seanchaí*, the traditional storyteller who gathered generations of people around the fireside and entertained them long into the night with legends, anecdotes and folktales.

"An actor doing a one-man show is very much in the tradition of the Irish storyteller," observes Dublin actor Eamon Morrissey, who has mounted three solo programs. "A one-man show is the twentieth century version of the *seanchaí*."

Micheál Mac Liammóir in *The Importance of Being Oscar*. "He would have dominated the English-speaking theatre if he had ever chosen to leave Ireland," observed his protégé, Orson Welles.

Micheál Mac Liammóir (1899-1978), who co-founded the Dublin Gate Theatre in 1928 and dominated the Irish theatrical scene for half a century, revived both tradition and his own acting career with his first solo performance. *The Importance of Being Oscar* brought Mac Liammóir the international recognition his patriotism had long denied him, and ignited the trend toward one-man shows in Ireland.

Drawing upon "this Godawful gift of gab" he felt afflicted him by birthright, Mac Liammóir brought Oscar Wilde back to life and evoked the spirit of an era which — as he suggested — Wilde might have invented. His arrangement of the artist's poems, plays and letters, interwoven with incisive commentary, reaffirmed both men's talents; the show celebrated Wilde's genius and reflected on his tragic fate.

The actor toured Europe, the United States, South America, South Africa and Australia with the program, following its premiere at Dublin Theatre Festival in 1960. In his second recital, *I Must Be Talking to My Friends,* Mac Liammóir "played host" to Ireland's druids, saints, wits and revolutionaries; *Talking About Yeats* was a tribute to the poet who inspired him during his formative years. Though *Friends* was perhaps his favorite of the three, *Oscar* was the most successful.

"Mac Liammóir was so subtly perceptive that his audiences lived with equal vividness through the glitter of Wilde's success and the torment of his disgrace," asserted theatre critic Desmond Rushe. "No one-man show since has succeeded in being so total in its rich accomplishment, and it is doubtful if any ever will."

Max Adrian as Shaw in *By George*, seen in London as *An Evening with GBS*.

Actor-playwright-designer Mac Liammóir — who has been called "a latter day Oscar Wilde, only more accomplished," by Gate Theatre alumnus Carroll O'Connor — depicted the great man of letters without physically portraying him. His director and lifelong associate, Hilton Edwards, decided in rehearsal that Mac Liammóir's role should be limited to that of biographer.

"As the project took shape I became convinced that... at no moment should the actor *play*, that is to say impersonate, Oscar Wilde. He could identify himself with Wilde's theories and emotions; he could temporarily become the characters of Wilde's creation, but he must never attempt to *be* Wilde," noted Edwards, who felt Mac Liammóir had to maintain the objectivity of the *seanchaí*. "Only then would he be able to establish intimacy with his audience; to forge a link between them and his subject and still be able to comment."

Edwards, who directed all three of Mac Liammóir's recitals, took a different approach in 1964 when he directed Bramwell Fletcher in *The Bernard Shaw Story*. Costumed in Norfolk jacket, tweed knickers and Shavian beard, the British actor bore substantial resemblance to the venerable Irish dramatist. Fletcher's portrait was no mere imitation, however; it drew upon a lifelong preoccupation with the playwright, whom he had met when he was 16.

Max Adrian, who also met Shaw on a few occasions, appeared in a subsequent Shavian entertainment devised by Michael Voysey. A veteran actor with experience in both classics and light comedy, Adrian was Irish-born, like Shaw. But *By George* reinforced the British stereotype of the Irish by focusing on GBS the comedian, at the expense of everything else. "There was no drama," complained critic William Goldman, who called the 1967 Broadway production "fatally predictable" and "a genuinely dreary evening."

A decade later, Donal Donnelly toured in Voysey's *My Astonishing Self* as a less acerbic and more humane Shaw, able to laugh at himself before making fun of someone else. Like Adrian, he played both the young, red-bearded rebel and the doddering, grey-whiskered patriarch; the characterization was not always convincing, but his Shaw had compassion as well as wit.

There were times when Donnelly was almost intimidated by the role. "I found that the more I read about Shaw the more colossal he seemed to be. I feel like an upstart at times and the more I think of the size of the man the more defeated I feel," the Dublin-born actor confessed in 1978. "But I hope [I] convey a side of Shaw that most people don't recognize."

Shay Duffin's evocation of Brendan Behan is easily recognizable, and saturated with authenticity — two pints of Guinness stout per performance. Behan's fondness for booze was the only qualification the actor felt he lacked when he cast himself in the role. The fact that they both

Shay Duffin quaffs real Guinness stout in his stage portrayal of
Brendan Behan but prefers non-alcoholic beverages offstage: "I
only drink when I'm working."

The Odyssey Theatre Ensemble

came from Dublin "enabled me to understand the character and why he viewed the world the way he did," Duffin has written. "Besides, we both had the same map-of-Ireland face, and both our figures were of the same sack-of-pota-toes-tied-in-the-middle variety."

Duffin's *Confessions of an Irish Rebel* — a showcase of Behan's writings, lectures and social comment — is as popular as it is robustly entertaining. The 47-year-old actor calculates he has given over 3,800 performances since the show's inauspicious premiere in a Canadian discotheque in 1971; he toured eight months in 1988 alone.

"When I decided to do Brendan as a one-man show, the earth had not settled" on his grave, Duffin reflects. "People had not gotten over the shock of the real thing. But it turned out my timing was perfect. People didn't want to get over the shock. They didn't want him to die."

Behan's larger-than-life personality has been immortalized in several solo shows. Ulick O'Connor's *Brendan* was far more judgmental than Duffin's show; based on O'Connor's biography of Behan, the program mingled sadness with humor in its depiction of a sensitive soul trying to live up to the coarse caricature of him created by the media. Niall Toibin's recital explored the theme of confusion in the individual and society; Michael Kavanaugh's more recent *Bein' With Behan* treads much the same ground as Duffin's *Confessions* but is more revealing of the writer's self-destructive nature.

While Behan and Shaw have become the most frequently impersonated Irish writers, Samuel Beckett — whose predilection for privacy is legend — has never been portrayed on stage. His work, however, seems to have inspired more one-man shows than any other twentieth century author.

When actor Jack MacGowran first compiled an anthology from Beckett's novels and plays in 1962, including excerpts from *Waiting for Godot* and *Endgame,* the author was less than wholly satisfied. In its final shape and form, however, *Beginning to End* achieved a harmony rarely present in one-man shows. "Author and actor are so commonly rooted in spirit that if Beckett were an actor he would be MacGowran, if MacGowran were a writer he would be Beckett," reasoned *New York Times* critic Mel Gussow. "It is an evening in the presence of two consummate artists exactly in tune with each other."

Billie Whitelaw, another performer on the same wavelength with the reclusive author, put together a one-woman show comprised of *Rockaby* and *Footfalls* — two one-acts written for her by Beckett — and a dramatic reading of *Enough.* "He always seems to be writing the story of my life," the English actress observed in a recent interview.

"I always seem to be on the stage on my own — if ever there's a speech more than 10 pages long at the Royal Shakespeare Company, it's flung in my direction," notes Whitelaw, who says long monologues give her a feeling of power. "You're out there on your own, and help cometh from nowhere. It is the biggest battle. I tap it."

Beckett tapped into his own *oeuvre* for the one-character play, *Company.* After it was published as a novella in 1980, there were several productions; finally, Beckett himself did a stage adaptation in collaboration with French director Pierre Chabert and American director S.E. Gontarski. Alan Mandell starred in the English language premiere.

Siobhán McKenna revived her career in 1970 by paying tribute to Irish authors in *Here Are Ladies*.

Actor Frederick Neumann, who appeared in his own version of *Company*, adapted Beckett's prose piece, *Worstward Ho*, for one performer — himself. To further maintain his singular concept, he also directed the 1987 New York production, which critic Mel Gussow called "a worthy addition to Beckett's theatrical body of work... in effect, a 'found' play." Neumann set the piece in a graveyard, planting himself knee-deep in a tomb, in a long tradition of truncated and disembodied Beckett protagonists.

Siobhán McKenna (1922-1986) similarly buried herself up to her waist in a mound of earth, to play the incurably optimistic heroine of Beckett's *Happy Days*, in a segment of her acclaimed one-woman show. While she did Beckett no disservice — and showed an appreciation for his facility with language — McKenna was more in tune with W.B. Yeats, Sean O'Casey, James Stephens and other authors she anthologized in *Here Are Ladies*.

"I love all our writers because they spoil you. If you are brought up on a diet of Irish writers, other writing seems a famine by comparison," said McKenna. "The old Gaelic literature was marvelously honest and Rabelaisian and yet had a spiritual content."

McKenna captured that spirituality in a dialogue between Mary and Christ on the cross, in Gaelic. She celebrated the Irish affinity for words with a recital of Yeats' "Crazy Jane" poems and a speech from Shaw's *St. Joan* — her best known role — in a voice one critic described as "thick and warm as an Irish wool blanket."

Devoting the second half of her show to James Joyce, McKenna brought *Ulysses* — and the eternally frustrated Molly Bloom — to exuberant life under Sean Kenny's direction. Tossing and turning in bed, she gave a virtuoso performance of Molly's long, erotic soliloquy, ruminating about her ambivalence toward sex and longing for her man "...or anyone."

The stream-of-consciousness monologue also served as the focal point of Fionnula Flanagan's later one-woman show, *James Joyce's Women*. Flanagan bore less physical resemblance to Molly than McKenna, but her performance was far more earthy — squatting on the chamber pot, lolling naked in bed, caressing her breasts, masturbating — too earthy for some. While there were those who felt it was "a serious breach of character," Flanagan steadfastly defended her interpretation.

Fionnula Flanagan contemplates love and sex as Molly Bloom in the film version of *James Joyce's Women*.

"It always seemed to me that a woman alone in her own bed at night, talking about her lover, her body, her sexuality, would look at her body while she is talking about it," the actress told an interviewer. *Los Angeles Times* critic Sylvie Drake called the scene "a rare and absolute victory over craft. Flanagan's Molly Bloom goes beyond performance to become, above all, an act of uncommon courage."

Although Flanagan was wary of doing the show in Dublin — because the Irish feel so strongly about Joyce — she courageously took it "home" for the Joyce Centenary in 1982. Her first introduction to the writer, as a Dublin schoolgirl, had impressed her more like "reading about my neighbors" than as great literature.

Flanagan became better acquainted with the author when she was cast as the sex-starved Gerty MacDowell in Joseph Strick's 1967 film version of *Ulysses*. Six years later the actress played Molly Bloom for the first time in Burgess Meredith's Broadway revival of *Ulysses in Nighttown* — which earned her a Tony nomination and inspired the solo program, also directed by Meredith.

Where McKenna's *Ladies* presented "women as seen through the eyes of Irish men," Flanagan's *Women* revealed the source of Joyce's uncanny insight into the female psyche. Instead of drawing on his imagination, the author questioned his wife Nora incessantly. "He was voraciously interested in everything she thought and felt," asserts Flanagan. "It's my premise that from the one woman whom he loved all his life, he then drew the skeletons and indeed the flesh and bones for many of his female characters."

In addition to Nora, Molly and Gerty, Flanagan portrayed the Washerwoman from *Finnegan's Wake* and two other real-life women — bookshop proprietor Sylvia Beach, who published *Ulysses*, and editor Harriet Weaver Shaw. When the show became a film in 1985 — with peripheral characters and flashbacks — the actress performed almost a one-woman show *behind* the scenes, functioning as screenwriter, producer and financier; the movie was filmed on a shoestring budget of less than $1 million.

While the economic advantages of solo theatre are no less apparent to the Irish than other nationalities, it is also a form well suited to the Celtic sense of individualism. "It's easier to mount a one-man show," maintains Eamon Morrissey, who assembled the first of his three solo programs in 1973 from the works of Irish humorist Myles na Gopaleen. "I had not intended *The Brother* to be a one-man show, but in the long run it was easier to do it myself than explain it to a lot of people."

Morrissey followed the huge success of the program with *Joycemen* — based on characters from *Ulysses* — and *Mr. Gulliver's Bag*, derived from Jonathan Swift. "A good one-man show releases the audience's imagination," he observes. "It's completely exhausting for the actor, mentally and physically, but it's also a great high."

There is also the downside, of course. "You are your own dancing master — there is no one else to throw you a line and no one to blame but yourself," concedes Shay Duffin. "But what God-fearing, silver-tongued, blathering Irishman who ever chipped a tooth kissing the Blarney Stone would think of such pitfalls?" he says. "My only complaint about my one-man show... is that the cast parties are lousy."

LONGACRE THEATRE

MIKE MERRICK and DON GREGORY

present

JULIE HARRIS

in

THE BELLE OF AMHERST

A New Play
Based on the life
of
Emily Dickinson

by
WILLIAM LUCE

Compiled by
TIMOTHY HELGESON

Scenery & Lighting **H. R. POINDEXTER**	*Costume Design by* **THEONI V. ALDREDGE**
Hair Design by **RAY IAGNOCCO**	*Production Supervisor* **GEORGE ECKERT**

General Manager
JAMES AWE

Directed by
CHARLES NELSON REILLY

A Dome/Creative Image Production

Emily, Charlotte, Zelda and Lillian

A word is dead
When it is said,
Some say.
I say it just
Begins to live
That day.

The Belle of Amherst was a warm, imaginative one-character play that brought one of America's best loved poets — and her words — back to life. The show did far more, however, than revivify Emily Dickinson; it enhanced two theatrical careers already in high gear and launched a third. It gave the versatile Julie Harris one of her most memorable roles to date, served notice that comedian Charles Nelson Reilly was to be taken seriously — as a director — and established William Luce as a playwright.

Unlike Harris and Reilly, Luce was a virtual non-entity when *The Belle* bowed on Broadway in 1976. The success of his first play — the first of four one-woman biographical dramas he has written to date — propelled Luce into a challenging career, for which he had no training.

But Luce had a propensity for switching vocations. As a young man, he studied classical music; by the age of 15, he was a professional pianist and a published poet. Following a 12-year stint as a minister — during which he also became an ASCAP composer-lyricist — he turned singer, performing with the Norman Luboff Choir and other groups.

When Reilly first approached Luce to script the Dickinson project, his instinct was to take a university course. "But there wasn't time. I learned through the doing of it," Luce stated in a recent interview. "When *The Belle* offer came, I had to jump on and act far more confident than I really was. The confidence has come since then."

Julie Harris herself lacked confidence when she first met Charles Nelson Reilly during the pre-Broadway tour of the 1965 musical, *Skyscraper;* "just the thought of getting up and singing and dancing petrified me," she later recalled. Reilly, her co-star, assured her everything would be all right. When Harris did an evening of readings from Dickinson as a benefit, during the lengthy run of the show, everything was more than all right.

"When the curtain came down at a production that had no planning, except the reading of a loose-leaf arrangement of poems and letters, I sat as transfixed as if I had watched Arthur Miller's *Death of a Salesman,*" asserted Reilly. "I realized I was in the presence of perhaps the most beautiful words I had ever heard." Notes Luce: "He saw theatricality as well as art in them. He said, 'Those words belong on a stage.'"

Years passed before Harris and Reilly teamed up to realize that jointly-held dream. By then Reilly had gone into business producing radio commercials with writer-director Timothy Helgeson, who would provide the necessary mortar by introducing the comedian and the actress to another Dickinson aficionado — his friend Bill Luce.

The future playwright arrived at their first meeting in a Hollywood studio commissary "carrying two shopping bags of books on Emily Dickinson. I spread them all out,"

Julie Harris as Emily Dickinson, and playwright William Luce, who wrote *The Belle of Amherst* and *Brontë* for her.

remembers Luce. "Julie had read them all. It was then that I realized how deep was her commitment to Dickinson."

Luce's first effort was a scenario for a television movie, which became a multi-character screenplay with the help of film director Lee Philips. A number of potential sponsors, including Hallmark, rejected the project. It was reborn in a New York night spot when Reilly met producers Mike Merrick and Don Gregory — who had just presented Henry Fonda as *Clarence Darrow* — and was told they were looking for a one-woman play. Replied Reilly: "How about Julie Harris as Emily Dickinson?"

Harris and Luce were intimately acquainted with the

nineteenth century poet by this point. But while the celebrated actress knew her craft inside and out — and had won four Tony awards and a flock of other laurels — the fledgling scribe was not at all sure of himself. He had seen Cornelia Otis Skinner and Agnes Moorehead in solo shows years earlier, and recalled them fondly, but when Merrick and Gregory asked him to turn his multi-character script into a one-woman play, he replied, "I don't know how to write a one-woman play."

In dramatizing Dickinson's life, Luce says, he "began to learn about the possibilities and limitations of monodrama. It was a matter of discovering my way, being imaginative. There were no classes to take, no books to read. A talented, creative director and a great actress were my first teachers."

Instead of reading about the art of monodrama, Luce read endlessly about Dickinson — as did Harris, Reilly and Tim Helgeson, his fellow members in "The Emily Committee." The script became a group effort after the playwright completed two drafts, the first of which the producers judged "too literary, too lyrical."

Luce put his subconscious to work on the rewrite. "I remember lying down for a nap... I dreamed that Julie walked out on a stage, and she was dressed in white. She carried flowers, stepped forward and said to the audience, 'Forgive me if I'm frightened. I never see strangers and hardly know what I say.' And then I woke up," recalls the playwright. "I wrote almost non-stop from that moment."

The words — which derived from a true account Luce had read — became the opening of the play. Emily then welcomed visitors to Amherst, introduced herself as "Squire Dickinson's half-cracked daughter," explained why she always dressed in white — to give the village gossips "something to talk about" — mimicked a nosy neighbor, and shared her recipe for black cake with the audience: "two pounds of flour, two pounds of sugar, two pounds of butter, nineteen eggs..."

By the time she finished reciting the ingredients, the stereotype of the shy, eccentric recluse had deserted the theatre. Harris and Luce had replaced her with a courageous and sensitive woman of childlike exuberance, in love with life and language — a vibrant wit who chose words with precision.

The inclusion of the recipe was no accident. "What could be less poetic? Or more startling? We are charmed by this earnest creature so anxious to share good things with us. Our lingering preconceptions about the remote Emily have vanished," observed theatre critic William B. Collins. "We're hooked. There is no resisting that cake."

Several critics, however, resisted the show's rich offerings, culinary and otherwise, when *The Belle of Amherst* opened on April 28, 1976 at the Longacre Theatre after a brief pre-Broadway tour. "It's a trick play, being written for a single actress, but the tricks are cheating," complained *New York* magazine's Alan Rich, "because conversations do take place and the one-character format is stretched and falsified constantly."

If the early reviews were negative, both the critics and the public soon took the play — and its affable heroine — to heart. The show was scheduled to run four weeks on Broadway; it ran five months. *New York Times* reviewer Walter Kerr called it "the most stimulating event of the season." Jack Kroll of *Newsweek* lauded its star for a performance "astonishing in its sagacity and passion."

"With her technical ability and her emotional range,

Miss Harris can convey profound inner turmoil at the same time that she displays an irrepressible gaiety of spirit," noted Edwin Wilson of *The Wall Street Journal*. "For those who cherish Miss Harris's unique gifts, this is a perfect opportunity to see her in a role perfectly suited for her."

Harris, who made her Broadway debut at 19 on a leave of absence from Yale, had found many such roles in the course of her much-honored career. At 24, she dazzled audiences as Frankie Addams, the 12-year-old tomboy, in *The Member of the Wedding;* she went on to capture Tony awards as the hedonistic Sally Bowles in *I Am a Camera*, a luminous Joan of Arc in Anouilh's *The Lark*, a chic divorcee in *Forty Carats*, and a disturbed President's widow in *The Last of Mrs. Lincoln*.

But the diminutive actress — whose radiant portrayal of Emily Dickinson won her a fifth Tony — had her doubts about the one-woman show. "It was the first time I'd ever had this kind of monumental studying to do. I just couldn't envision it. I thought, they'll have to give me at least a year to even memorize it," recalled Harris. "That was really the greatest fear I had in the whole project — not so much that I was going to be on the stage alone, but that I was so afraid that I would not be able to remember."

Harris, who managed to "stuff those words into my head" in three months, had a decisive advantage; she had already been associated with the poet who viewed words as "entities" for nearly 20 years, beginning with the first of two Caedmon albums of poems and letters. When a 40-minute high school guest appearance once stretched into a three-hour reading of Dickinson's work — and stopped the school bells — she made TV news headlines. Everyone was surprised but Harris: "To me, she was like a thunderbolt."

Bill Luce, who was first struck by that thunderbolt as a high school student, came to know Dickinson chiefly through her letters, which radiated "an invisible light... a mystical energy." The play he would eventually write, based largely on those letters, "illuminated the things she's felt in her heart," observed Harris. "It reflects every lifetime. In that way, it would seem like a concerto, or a piece of music."

Though he did not originally conceive *The Belle* as a monodrama, the musician-turned-playwright was quick to tune into the harmony of the approach. "I consider the one-person play to be uniquely suited to the telling of Emily's story. She was seclusive, an individualist of the highest order," says Luce. It was most appropriate that "Emily alone should tell her story, sharing with the audience the inner drama of a poet's consciousness in an intimate, one-to-one relationship."

Charles Nelson Reilly was perhaps the least likely individual to be associated with such intimate material. Yet despite his rubber face and high-pitched guffaw — and his "anything for a laugh" reputation sustained by years of musical comedies and TV game shows — he was a bonafide member of the creative team.

"You might think, how could one stay for five sane minutes in a room with such a person let alone be directed by him in a play about Emily Dickinson," conceded Harris. "But under Charles' clown facade beats a heart so sensitive to the psychology of what an actor is all about and what audiences respond to... appearances can be deceiving."

Reilly brought his outrageous sense of fun to the project along with his sensitivity. It was not an inappropriate contribution. "Emily Dickinson had a great sense of humor;

that's why I, being a comedian, was always attracted to her work," he observed. "Some of her poems are like special pieces of material you could do in Las Vegas!" Harris concurred: "How could you read her work and not know she was humorous?"

Wry humor was an essential ingredient when Harris, Luce and Reilly subsequently reteamed on a another biographical drama. The idea for a play on Charlotte Brontë — a favorite author of both Harris and Dickinson — came about when Boston's public broadcasting station, WGBH, invited the actress to do something of her own choosing for Masterpiece Radio Theatre.

Harris was asked to write the play, but thought it wiser to turn the job over to Luce. "It was to be a two-hour play, and I said, 'Maybe we should have several characters in this,'" recalls the playwright. "She replied, 'Then I won't do it.' So a second one-woman play was born." It was entitled *Currer Bell, Esq.* — Brontë's nom de plume.

The actress felt "Charlotte should be the one to tell the story" rather than sisters Anne and Emily — partly because the author of *Jane Eyre* left more extant letters, and "because she survived her sisters and brother and is able to give the greatest perspective on the Brontë family."

Elinor Stout's production won several broadcasting awards, including the prestigious Peabody. The program was then recorded for Caedmon and filmed as *Brontë* for Irish television, with Delbert Mann directing on location in rural County Wicklow (standing in for Brontë's Yorkshire).

But Harris was "aching to do it on the stage," and asked Luce to rework the play for her. Reilly signed on as director, and the show "got transformed into a lively theatre piece," says Luce. "I went through the re-creating process

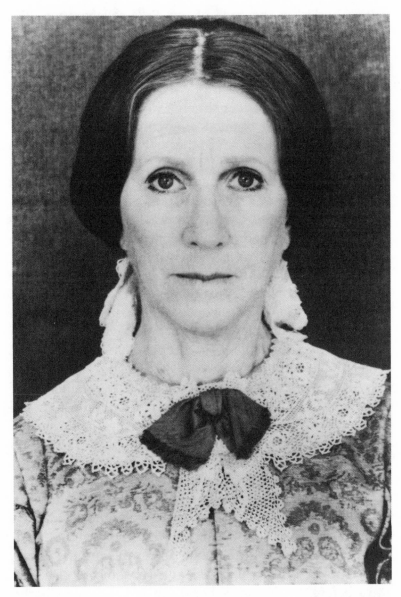

Julie Harris as *Brontë*, which began as a radio play and was filmed for Irish television before its transformation into a stage play.

with Charles, in the style of our *Belle* collaboration. The play took on a new identity."

Harris gave the first stage presentation of *Brontë* as a benefit for Hollywood's Matrix Theatre in 1983. The demands of her regular role on TV's *Knots Landing* limited her subsequent performances largely to one-night stands. More recently, she commissioned playwright Donald Freed — author of *Secret Honor* and other one-person shows — to write a third solo program for her; *Countess*, which featured Harris as the wife of Count Leo Tolstoy, had its premiere in 1986 as a benefit for her church.

Luce, meanwhile, went on to write two additional one-woman shows — and a multi-character play in which he poked fun at himself as an author of monodramas. In 1979, entrepreneur Lane Yorke commissioned him to write a play about the schizophrenic wife of novelist F. Scott Fitzgerald. When Luce read Zelda Fitzgerald's private letters, which Yorke sent him on microfilm — and discovered "a woman different from the shallow stereotype we've come to know" — he plunged into the project.

After Yorke performed in an amateur production of *Zelda* at the Piccolo Spoleto Festival in Charleston, S.C., the rights reverted to Luce. In 1984, the late Olga Bellin starred in a well-received off-Broadway production. Two years later, the actress for whom the part was apparently meant all along entered the picture, in the person of Piper Laurie.

The veteran performer, best known for roles in such films as *The Hustler* and *Carrie,* had been approached years earlier with a short one-character piece on Fitzgerald. Laurie went to New York to obtain approval from the estate, only to find the rights had been given to someone else "just days before" — Yorke. When Luce and director Charles

Nelson Reilly offered her the role in 1986, she learned the playwright had thought of her when he first wrote the drama, due to the physical resemblance between them.

At the Burt Reynolds Theatre in Jupiter, Florida, where Reilly is artistic director, he and Luce completely reworked the play about the tragic one-time symbol of The Jazz Age and retitled it *The Last Flapper*. Laurie's input was invaluable to the process. The playwright and the director — whom Luce describes as "my secret ingredient" — continued to tinker with the show, even while the actress toured in the role.

By the time he tackled his third one-woman play, Luce was being inundated with offers to script solo biographical dramas on poets, politicians and movie stars. He turned them all down. Instead, he wrote a TV movie called *The Last Days of Patton* for George C. Scott — and a cast of hundreds.

The playwright was finally persuaded to create a fourth monodrama, based on the memoirs of Lillian Hellman, by producers Ann and Bob Shanks. "I had vowed not to write another one-person play," says Luce. "I wanted to work in new areas and have other challenges. Yet, the offer intrigued me because I'd be working with Miss Hellman personally."

At their first meeting, the controversial writer told Luce, "You and I are natural enemies." Long an admirer of both Hellman's literary achievements and moral ideals, he found he did not have to "trespass on her words" or dramatize incidents in the subject's life, as he had for his previous plays. The former victim of the blacklist "had already done it in her books," says Luce. "She prepared her life for dramatic portraiture."

The colorful iconoclast admired Luce's integrity but disapproved of the solo concept, and had him write in five additional characters who would drift in and out as they were called up from memory. Hellman also had casting approval, and apparently "wanted herself played by a movie goddess," says Luce, who found that fact "touching and sad." Faye Dunaway, Barbra Streisand and Jane Fonda — who portrayed her in the film, *Julia* — were among her choices.

Hellman's casting ideas, along with the "dream characters," died with her when she succumbed in 1984. Luce then suggested veteran Australian actress Zoe Caldwell — a recent Tony winner for *Medea* — for the role; her husband, renowned producer Robert Whitehead, was asked to direct. Both accepted, and Whitehead reinstated the original one-woman approach.

Giving birth to *Lillian* was a painful experience for Caldwell, who experienced severe loneliness and "morning sickness" throughout the long gestation period. "Part of it had to do with being the one person in a play," she told *The New York Times*. "Part of it had to do with not wanting to let Lillian into me... [she] is a difficult person to have inhabit you." When Caldwell phoned a mutual friend, actress Maureen Stapleton, to tell her of the agony, Stapleton laughed and said, "She'd be so-o-o-o happy."

Luce was happy when the play opened on Broadway in 1986, after a successful run in Washington D.C., and then toured — not because the show garnered glowing notices, but because "controversy attended it everywhere." The conservative *Washington Times* used their review to attack Hellman — who made many more enemies than friends during her life — as "one of the great liars of the age" and

insisted that her memoirs were fictionalized or grossly dis-
torted. Many New York critics also felt the play was
"whitewashed" because it based on the subject's reminiscences — notably *Scoundrel Time,* her pungent memoir of
the McCarthy era.

"The controversy was the stuff playwrights' dreams are
made of," says Luce, noting that *Lillian* has already been
optioned in more countries than *The Belle of Amherst,* which
preceded it by a decade. "The political element is the attrac-
tion, I believe. Every time her name is mentioned, a barrage
of verbal artillery goes off. Lillian would've loved it."

Luce's work has aroused controversy from the beginning. Critics have quarreled over whether his one-character
creations are really "plays" and debated his dramatic de-
vices; scholars have derided him for taking liberties with
the facts.

"Anyone's life put factually onto the stage would be
stupefyingly dull," asserts Luce. "It's as Emily Dickinson
said, 'Tell all the truth, but tell it slant.' When I wrote *The
Belle* ...I found I had to make choices that might not be
provable, to make the thing stageworthy. Her life was an
enigma to begin with. To believe that a playwright must
construct a drama on Dickinson or Hellman or anyone else
out of facts only, is to begin with an erroneous premise."
Hellman was so contemporary and so widely known, however, that "such liberties, even in the theatre, were unten-
able."

According to Luce, the traditional ground rules for writing a play also apply to the monodrama. But he admits to
making up his own rules when the situation called for it,
and breaking them when he chose. "I believe that what
emerged in *The Belle* was a fresh concept for solo perform-

Piper Laurie as Zelda Fitzgerald in *The Last Flapper*, "a gifted woman who was born into the wrong generation and married to the wrong man," namely F. Scott Fitzgerald.

ers. I felt it was truly a *play* for one person, that it functioned as a play functions," he states. While he concedes that "a few critics bristled at calling it a play," he is not overly concerned with labels. "To me... play, show, monologue, monodrama — call it what you like... if the audience is engaged emotionally, intellectually, I'm happy."

The device which allows a performer to address the audience from time to time — as employed by Luce and other creators of monodrama — has also caused commotion. "While audiences accept this practice readily, it is only the occasional critic who complains about it," observes the playwright. "In their eyes, the audience must have an identity. I do understand this concern, although I see one-person plays work wonderfully without giving a face to people in the dark. Yet, I do have my Emily Dickinson speak to the audience as a visitor in her parlor." In *Lillian*, the audience is a visitor in a hospital waiting room; in *Brontë*, Luce made no dispensation for theatregoers whatsoever: "they're on their own."

As for *The Last Flapper*, "I figured Zelda was a schizophrenic and could talk to the air, if she pleased." Even with that premise, one critic took the practitioner of one-person shows to task for failing to solve what he called "the basic problem of the genre: making it clear who the protagonist is talking to, and why." When actress Piper Laurie asked Luce to consider the issue, the playwright talked it over with Charles Nelson Reilly and decided that Fitzgerald could be talking to a fellow patient at the mental institution.

Another controversial device is the means by which Luce sometimes calls up the past — having his protagonist address unseen characters onstage. In *The Belle of Amherst*,

Photo by Joan Marcus

Zoe Caldwell as *Lillian*, the rebellious writer who refused to "cut my conscience to fit this year's fashions" during the height of the McCarthy era.

Julie Harris pulled off such difficult stunts by virtue of her personality. But there were those who felt the scene in *Brontë* where she addressed her invisible Papa in an empty chair strained credibility.

In *Lillian*, "the actress has become a storyteller totally. I think now I like that approach the best," says Luce. "If I were ever to write another one-person play, I wouldn't have unseen characters whose retorts the audience would be left to figure out. I like having the actor inform us of everything."

With each one-character play, observes Luce, the art of writing solo has become "deceptively simpler, in that I now know how to do it, but I have to *not* do it that way. So it's harder to be different." Although each character is different, he says, "I find I have to locate a new center to work from."

The writer does not take his work so seriously that he cannot have fun with it. In 1985 he concocted a spoof about a playwright, not unlike himself, who is visited by his muses — the subjects of his first four one-woman plays — while he is struggling with a fifth. In the course of *Luce Women*, Lillian Hellman introduces Charlotte Brontë to Marlboro cigarettes, while Zelda Fitzgerald teaches Emily Dickinson how to dance the Charleston.

Lantern Theatre

38 Merrion Square

PRESENTS

JACK MacGOWRAN

IN

BEGINNING TO END

A PERFORMANCE OF WORK BY

SAMUEL BECKETT

Homage to Beckett

The works of Samuel Beckett lend themselves uniquely to the theatre of the individual. His novels, prose pieces and multi-character plays more often than not appear to take place inside the human mind, making many of them logical for adaptation as solo theatre. He himself has made a number of expeditions into the territory with a series of monologues and one-character vignettes, beginning with *Krapp's Last Tape*.

Despite the author's legendary refusal to adapt his works to mediums other than those for which they were written — or permit others to do so — he allowed two dedicated actors to transform his novels, plays and poetry into one-man shows. Jack MacGowran changed forever the public perception of Beckett, from a purveyor of gloom and despair to a writer of wit and humanity; a generation later, Barry McGovern has further enhanced the author's reputation.

MacGowran (1918-1973), a veteran of Ireland's Abbey and Gate Theatres, was more closely associated with the plays of Sean O'Casey when he devised the first such monodrama. He was already well acquainted with Beckett, however, having appeared in Britain's first English-language presentation of *Endgame*, a TV version of *Waiting for Godot*, and the original BBC Radio productions of *All That Fall* and *Embers* — the latter written especially for him.

He possessed a singular talent and temperament well-suited to the demands of solo entertainment. He was a fine ensemble actor, but had difficulty sharing the stage with performers who lacked his split-second timing. When the role matched his abilities — Seamus Shields in O'Casey's *The Shadow of a Gunman*, Harry Hope in O'Neill's *The Iceman Cometh*, Clov in Beckett's *Endgame* — he could draw the audience to him like a magnetic force. But he was limited in the parts he could play, at least in the minds of producers and casting directors; his small stature and unusual appearance brought him more offers to play "little green men" than anything else.

MacGowran finally began to transcend the stereotype of the Stage Irishman — and alter Beckett's cheerless image — in the fall of 1962. A one-man Beckett anthology was not the first project that came to mind when MacGowran was asked to do something for the Dublin Theatre Festival, nor was it the actor's idea; his wife Gloria was the one who suggested it.

The concept appealed immediately to MacGowran, but not in the manner she had intended. "My idea was to change people's ideas about Jack, to show the different facets of things he could do. We chose things that would show the range he had. It was a totally selfish thing on my part," recalled Gloria MacGowran. "But Jack wanted to show the beauty and the humor in Sam; that was his concern."

MacGowran called the author and asked for his approval, then went to Paris to discuss the project. Beckett was delighted with the idea. The actor chose *Act Without Words I*, the author's elaborate "mime for one player," as the basic framework for the show. He also selected an excerpt from the seminal novel, *Molloy*; a long, convoluted monologue from *Waiting for Godot*; a speech from *Endgame*;

a passage from *Krapp's Last Tape;* and the short prose piece, *From an Abandoned Work,* in its entirety.

The late Donald McWhinnie, who had directed the actor in the radio productions of *All That Fall* and *Embers* — and had first introduced MacGowran to Beckett at the actor's timid request in 1957 — directed the program. Alluding to Beckett's preoccupation with nightfall, MacGowran called the program *End of Day.*

The show was rehearsed on an irregular basis, inbetween jobs, "an hour here, an hour there, over a period of months," McWhinnie recalled in an interview. "Artistically it wasn't really satisfactory. Jack didn't have the texts down, he hadn't mastered the words... gradually he came around to an awareness of things. The project wasn't too well conceived, but it was a kind of starting point. It needed a lot more thought and working out."

MacGowran's lone, black-clad, bowler-hatted figure was the hit of the theatre festival when *End of Day* premiered in Dublin on October 5, 1962. The Gaiety Theatre was filled to capacity for his one-night stand. "Mr. MacGowran demolished once and for all the caricature of Beckett as a gloomy, obscure dramatist of dustbins, deformity and despair," declared Alec Reid in *The Irish Times.*

MacGowran's decision to depart from the pantomime of *Act Without Words,* speaking passages of text and then returning to it, aroused much controversy when he appeared in London. Beckett, who had seen the show in rehearsal but had no input on the script, was unhappy with the way MacGowran had used the pantomime. He gently told the actor, "A mime is served best without words."

In the year that followed his first attempt at putting

Photo by Joseph Abeles

Jack MacGowran in the 1970 New York Shakespeare Festival
production of his one-man Beckett anthology.

together a one-man show, MacGowran began to develop a far deeper appreciation of Beckett's spare and elusive work. In 1963, while the actor was directing a play in Paris, they met on several occasions. They talked less about each other's work than they did about Dublin, where they had grown up only a few miles from each other; as their alliance grew, MacGowran decided that he could no longer act in anything of Beckett's without the man's supervision.

Early the following year in Paris, Beckett directed MacGowran in an English-language production of *Endgame* that soon transferred to London, and came to be regarded as definitive. Later in 1964 the author supervised a London revival of *Waiting for Godot,* which featured MacGowran as Lucky, the woebegone slave.

The following year, the actor revived his solo show at the Lantern Theatre in Dublin. *Beginning to End* was substantially different from *End of Day;* conspicuous by its absence was the frantic pantomime. At Beckett's suggestion, MacGowran discarded the stylized costume and whiteface makeup he had worn in the first production, and garbed himself in a large, shapeless black greatcoat. The first half of the show was now comprised of Beckett's poetry and passages from the novels, the second half excerpted primarily from plays. A theme began to take shape: "the feelings and thoughts of a man faced with death."

More than four years passed before MacGowran and Beckett would once more resurrect the monodrama and restructure it into its final form. By the time they reunited in Paris in 1970, Beckett had won the Nobel Prize for Literature and MacGowran had become an international film star of growing repute — and declining health.

Despite the demand for his talents by such filmmakers

as Roman Polanski and Peter Brook, MacGowran's devotion to the theatre, and to Beckett, was unrelenting. The bond was deep between them; both were Dublin born and Dublin bred, and both had fled their homeland when it threatened to suffocate them artistically. It was not an intellectual affinity they had but a spiritual affinity.

MacGowran was intimately acquainted with the characters that peopled Beckett's novels and plays. As a reformed alcoholic and a manic depressive, he identified with their dark souls in a way no other actor could. He recognized their black Irish humor because he had grown up with it; he knew their hoplessness because he had lived it.

But he also sensed the affirmation of life at the core of Beckett's work that had eluded others. Where critics and scholars were preoccupied by the nihilism and the despair, MacGowran was aroused by the writer's comic imagery, his courage — and, above all, his compassion for the human condition.

"No matter how you approach Beckett, through his novels or his plays, no matter what setting he places his characters in for dramatic purposes, never will they give way to despair," observed MacGowran. "The key word in all his plays is 'perhaps'... and therein lies the hope that there's a fifty-fifty chance of things going our way."

Beckett had never been entirely happy with MacGowran's concept of the one-man show, neither in its first manifestation as *End of Day*, nor in subsequent editions. Though MacGowran had sought — and received — Beckett's cooperation through all its incarnations, the anthology was still a work-in-progress not wholly satisfactory.

Jack MacGowran and Samuel Beckett, rehearsing for a 1965 TV production of *Beginning to End*.

As Beckett and MacGowran fine-tuned their portrait of a man "striving for the ability to come to terms with death, and still to laugh at himself" — as the actor described him — the character came into focus. In assimilating the novels, plays and poems, the actor had come to the realization that Beckett's characters were all of the same mind and marrow, the same steady, unmistakable voice. The unlikely protagonist of his show was a composite of all the deliciously eccentric old tramps who wandered the streets of their hometown, in the very same ankle-length greatcoat.

As his understanding of the author's work grew, MacGowran realized the misfits who peopled the Beckett landscape were blood brothers to the silent film comics they had both admired in their youth. When MacGowran asked Beckett how much laughter he expected from the show, the answer came readily: "As much as you can get." The stuff of Beckett was tragi*comedy*, not morbidity and despair. "People find Beckett morose," MacGowran said once in disbelief. "I find him *so* funny."

Few passages in modern literature, he felt sure, could be funnier than the sequence in *Molloy* in which the hero calculates with impeccable logic the circulation of 16 pebbles, transferring them among his pockets one by one, then four by four, and finally devises a mathematical progression of "sucks and transfers" in order to guarantee "not one sucked twice, not one left unsucked."

With the author's assistance, MacGowran pared tangential words and phrases, to make the texts more cohesive for presentation — the "sucking stones" sequence was eight pages long in the novel. At any length, the tongue-twisting structure of the monologues demanded an uncanny feat of memorization, perhaps more formidable than anything an actor of MacGowran's generation had ever tackled. He was almost paranoid about getting the words right, to an "and" and a "but"; it had to be absolutely correct at all times.

Beckett himself directed the show, dedicating himself as fully to the task as he had the creation of the words themselves. While he refused to take any credit for it, he was wholly in charge of the program. "His directions were deliberate and without a choice... He'd say, '*This* is the way *that* should go,'" MacGowran recalled. "There were long pauses of silence while Beckett looked to the floor. Then he said two or three sentences and the whole thing was clear."

The playwright, as per his custom, was nowhere to be

seen when *Beginning to End* opened in Paris on April 23, 1970. Instead he waited backstage with a warm embrace for his confrere. As usual, words between them were few. "Jack was like a brother," said Beckett later. "I didn't have to talk to him; I didn't have to direct him. He just *knew*."

That fall, the solo entertainment traveled to the U.S., where it was presented — as *Jack MacGowran in the Works of Samuel Beckett* — under the auspices of the New York Shakespeare Festival. The actor was afraid Beckett might be a writer of limited appeal in the United States, still a bit ahead of his time; Joseph Papp convinced him otherwise. Neither were prepared for the success that greeted the show, particularly the Obie award for Best Actor in an Off Broadway performance.

In Berlin — where the show caused a furor of the sort generally reserved for pop stars — the dramaturg of the Schiller-Theater asked Beckett for permission to do the show with a German actor. He was refused. "I don't want anyone else to do it except Jack," said the author. "No one else *could* do it but Jack."

When the foremost interpreter of Beckett's work died of heart disease early in 1973, *Beginning to End* died with him — or so it seemed, until a few years had passed. Jose Ferrer, a longtime friend of MacGowran's, then went to Beckett and asked for permission to do the show; the author agreed, on the condition that Ferrer did it a different way.

The actor put together a one-man potpourri that combined his own mini-version of *Acting Shakespeare*, post-Gielgud, pre-McKellen, with a Chekhov monologue and an appalling attempt at the "sucking stones" speech from *Molloy* — proving that Beckett was beyond his considerable talents.

English, Irish and American actors approached Gloria MacGowran for the rights to the anthology in the years that followed her husband's untimely death. She turned them all down, but sought out various performers on her own; plans were announced to reprise the show with Jack Lemmon but never came to fruition.

In 1984, Dublin actor Barry McGovern was asked if he would do a solo Beckett program for the Gate Theatre. Despite a lifelong fascination with the author's work — which began when he saw MacGowran in the BBC *Waiting for Godot* as a teenager — he was hesitant.

"I wasn't too keen on one-man shows," states McGovern, who began his career at the Abbey School of Acting. "I'd only seen three memorable ones, including *Beginning to End*. One of the reasons I was very reluctant to do it was the great memory of MacGowran, who was such a hero of mine. I said, 'No, I can't do it. It's already been done.'"

Gate Theatre director Michael Colgan was not easily discouraged. He persuaded McGovern there was a new generation who hadn't seen MacGowran — and that the young actor, who had appeared in five productions of *Endgame* and *Waiting for Godot* — was capable of the project. They discussed several options, including the likelihood of restaging *Beginning to End*. When they couldn't come to an agreement with Gloria MacGowran, Beckett suggested "the possibility of doing a different one-man show" with a different choice of texts, recalls McGovern.

Beckett's post-war trilogy of novels, *Molloy, Malone Dies* and *The Unnamable* — the core of his work — had always been a particular favorite of McGovern's: "I said, 'Why don't we just stick to the trilogy, and do a show based on that.' There's a such a goldmine there." In collaboration with Beckett scholar Gerry Dukes, the actor assembled a program and called it *I'll Go On*, after the final life-affirming words of *The Unnamable*: "...you must go on, I can't go on, I'll go on."

While McGovern did not use Beckett's poems or plays, there were overlaps with MacGowran's show, which featured several extracts from the trilogy. "The 'sucking stones' is too good to be left out. How could we not do it?" says McGovern, who lamented all the material he had to exclude. The first act of *I'll Go On* is a 55-minute condensation of *Molloy*; the shorter but more intense second act is taken primarily from *Malone Dies*, with the final minutes from *The Unnamable*. "We tried to get away from the phrase 'adapted by' — we didn't want to make it a dramatization of the trilogy because you can't really do that; we leave so much out. What we tried to do is give people a feeling in an hour and a half, the essence of what the novels are about," explains McGovern.

As MacGowran realized two decades earlier, the actor found he had to have the text down letter-perfect or he couldn't do it at all. McGovern, who has played a wide variety of classic and contemporary roles, thought it might be easy to memorize because the dense novels possessed a "perverted logic," but found it exceedingly difficult. Two and a half months were required to learn the script, followed by four weeks of rehearsal.

The show premiered on September 23, 1985, at the Dublin Theatre Festival. "I was never so terrified in my life," McGovern recalls of the opening night. "I was as well prepared as I could be, I knew the material; we'd worked like hell on it. But at the same time, it was just me going out

Barry McGovern in his adaptation of Beckett's post-war trilogy,
I'll Go On.

there in front of these people. Sheer terror got me through it. I don't know how I did it. You can bluff your way through something less… but if you go wrong in this show, you're finished."

McGovern, who thought the program might last six nights at the festival, has since taken the solo entertainment around Europe, to Israel and the U.S. While he is amazed at the success he has had with it, he says, he never takes it for granted. "The show is always an ordeal," he affirms. "It gets easier only in the sense that, once you've done something you know you can do it again. But it's always a mountain to climb."

Although he appears to climb that mountain alone, he insists he is part of an ensemble. "It's known as a one-man show, but it's no more that than the man in the moon," says McGovern, citing the set design contributed by Robert Ballagh, the lighting design of Rupert Murray and the direction of Colm O Briain.

The constant comparisons that have been made to Jack MacGowran since he began doing the show are "like an albatross," says the actor, who concedes they are inevitable. "But I take it with a grain of salt," claims McGovern. "I thought he was terrific, and I was a great admirer of his. I couldn't hope to do his show the way he did it; I wouldn't dream of even trying. Even if we had gotten permission to do it, it would have been done as a tribute to him."

Such a tribute was mounted in 1987 when Gloria MacGowran — a Beckett aficionado long before she met her late husband — directed a new production of *Beginning to End* in Toronto, Canada. The presentation, which starred David Fielder, won glowing reviews; one critic called it "an incredibly visceral, deeply affecting evening of theatre… a hypnotically powerful 90 minutes."

JACK AND RICHARD LAWRENCE
present

RAY STRICKLYN

as

TENNESSEE WILLIAMS

in

CONFESSIONS OF A NIGHTINGALE

Adapted by

**CHARLOTTE
CHANDLER** & **RAY
STRICKLYN**

Directed by

JOHN TILLINGER

Monologue: Ray Stricklyn

"My working habits are so very private," confides the man in the wicker chair, between sips of white wine. "I'd much prefer discussing with you the most intimate details of my sex life, because the work, to me, is more personal." And discuss them he does — but then, he warns his audience in the beginning he intends to simply "let it all hang out." "Everyone is always so titillated by sex — especially homosexuality — so let's get that little demon out in the open first. Am I homosexual? I don't know how that rumor got started... As I [said] on national TV, 'I cover the waterfront.'"

The words are pure Tennessee Williams — not the Williams of A Streetcar Named Desire and Cat on a Hot Tin Roof, but the strange and lonely man who — as he said himself — did publicly what other people did privately. Indeed, actor Ray Stricklyn's portrait of the famed playwright brings to mind George Orwell's description of Salvador Dalí's autobiography: "a striptease in pink limelight."

Confessions of a Nightingale does more than tease, however; it reveals its subject in rare candor. Offstage, the show's sole performer is equally candid about his own up-and-down life — and a dark period that not only parallels Williams' creative decline but was "necessary for my development."

Stricklyn, whose Broadway debut in The Climate of Eden garnered him an award as one of the "most promising" personalities of the 1952-53 season, was destined for fame and fortune in Hollywood — or so the Houston-born actor thought. "I was very

*young, and I looked even younger. I had about five or six wonder-
ful years as a juvenile; I thought I was on my way to being a
'star,'" he says. To his dismay, he was still playing teenagers at
age 35. "That's not an unusual story," he observes, "but I didn't
handle it too well."*

*"Things got more dire. I was drinking... then my father died.
My ambition and drive started to wane. I felt guilty over the
success I was having," reveals Stricklyn, who won a Golden
Globe nomination for his performance in* The Plunderers. *After
a wholly dissatisfying performance in Tennessee Williams'* Cam-
ino Real, *he quit acting; for several years he did menial labor
until a friend got him a part-time public relations job; the job
became a career, and he began to gain back his self respect.*

*When he ran into director Jose Quintero at a party and voiced
his desire to act again, he was invited to audit Quintero's workshop. But when an actress in the class asked him to audition for
the role of Nightingale in her production of Williams'* Vieux
Carre, *he balked. "I didn't think I was right for the role," recalls
Stricklyn. "Jose said, 'Why don't you do a scene in class?' It went
quite well, and he said, 'Ray, I think you could be wonderful in
this part.' His encouragement was all I needed." The production
won Stricklyn the Los Angeles Drama Critics Circle Award.*

*The solo program was born the following season, when the
Beverly Hills Playhouse approached him about doing a tribute to
honor the late playwright. "Milton Katselas had commissioned
an artist to do a bust of Tennessee," says Stricklyn, "and his
assistant, Eric Leonard, asked me if I would put together a program for the unveiling. I thought I'd do about 15 minutes of me as
Tennessee, and then have other actors do scenes from his plays.
The monologue got longer and longer, and ended up an hour
long; we never did the scenes."*

Confessions *opened at the Playhouse January 4, 1985. Since its triumphant Off Broadway run, it has toured the U.S. and traveled to Edinburgh. It has brought a flock of awards, reviews almost unanimous in their acclaim, and most important, a measure of hard-earned respect to its battle-scarred star.*

A one-man show is the hardest form of theatre. It's grueling, if you're in a long run situation, playing it every night and matinees as well. At least my piece is. It's so intimate and so inward; it's very draining emotionally. I wondered why, a day or so after I'd done the show, my body would just be aching all over; I thought, "Why? All I do is sit there." The tension that you're in for 90 minutes, it's as though you had done hard physical labor some place — the way you're using the mind, and concentrating, and the body tensing and all. You try to look relaxed — but it takes a tremendous toll on the body, let alone the memory.

Also, if you're successful with a show like this and you're fortunate enough to go on the road, it's very lonely. You don't have other actors to bitch with, or play with — you're on you own. You go to these strange towns; there may be an opening night party, but then you're basically on your own. A piece like this never quite leaves me. I can be out shopping, but if I know I have a show to do that night... the process is going through my head. I know the script, but I'm always thinking about it.

I was really nervous when I opened in Chicago. Tennessee Williams' brother, Dakin, was in the front row. I thought, "He's got a reputation more eccentric than Tennessee. He'll probably jump up and say, 'That's not the way it was.' But he couldn't have been sweeter to me afterwards. He was unhappy about one [statement] because he said it wasn't true — it was one of Tennessee's lies. I said, "I am doing Tennessee's story — not yours." Tennessee was very contradictory; like most of us, he dramatizes a story to make it more dramatic from his point of view.

The sexuality, if that offends some people — again, that's Tennessee. And he loved to shock people. I had things in it when I first started, some of his quotes, I cut. When he's talking about his first sexual experiences in school, now I say, "The only sexual encounters we had were sordid experiences with syphilitic old whores." The original line was much better. I did it for months, but it did offend a lot of people — it was gloriously phrased, but it was the most disgusting picture.

I can tell almost from the moment I walk out there what kind of audience I have. When I went to Santa Barbara [California] which is a pretty reserved community... I hadn't been out there 10 minutes when three elderly ladies got up and slowly went up the aisle. One of the critics said, "It's too bad they didn't stay. They would've learned something. But after all, they got Tennessee Williams, not John Wayne."

At times I think, well, maybe there's too much sex. If I were to rework the play, I'd cut some of it — and yet, I think my initial instincts were right because if I'm trying to do a psychological study on Tennessee, it was *such* a integrated and important part of his life. He was *such* a sexually-oriented man. He was constantly writing or thinking about sex... sex and death. And those are the main themes in my play. Although he says in the script, "I know, in my work, I've always had a fascination for death and a fascination for sexuality, but I wouldn't say they're my predominant theme. Loneliness is."

I met Tennessee when I first went to New York. He was at Circle in the Square, reading his poetry and scenes from his plays. It was sold out. I was standing there dejectedly and a short gentleman came up and asked if he could help me. I said, "I can't get a ticket." He said, "Follow me." Afterwards this man — producer Paul Bigelow — said, "Are you an actor?" I said yes. He said, "Well, you're very right for a role we're casting for Westport."

The play was about an older woman and a young boy; it was supposed to star Greer Garson. I took the subway to Bigelow's apartment. Tennessee was there... I thought, "Oh, Christ." I was scared enough without having Tennessee Williams hear me read. Paul suggested Tennessee read the Greer Garson role opposite my young man. At the end of the reading, he said, "Paul, I advise you to give the part to the young man." Miss Garson for whatever reason backed out; they eventually cancelled the whole project.

Tennessee later got me a job reading scripts for his agent, Audrey Wood. Then he was working on *Cat on a Hot Tin Roof* and needed script revisions, and I typed about a month, on and off, working on that. So I was around him — I can't say I knew him well. But I was very young and very naive, and I was in great awe — and he had this reputation and I was very... leery of that, but of course he was a perfect gentleman and never did anything.

I never had any dream that Mr. Williams would become an important factor in my career and life. He didn't really write plays for young men when I was a juvenile actor, so I never got to be in any of his plays. I always

Ray Stricklyn as Tennessee Williams in *Confessions of a Nightingale,* based on a no-holds-barred interview with the late playwright.

wanted to play Tom in *Glass Menagerie* but never got to. When I first went to New York, I auditioned at a drama school with a Williams' one-act, *Mooney's Kid Don't Cry* — and was fortunate enough to win a scholarship. In a way, Tennessee started my career, and then with my help ended it — then began it again.

Vieux Carré ran six months. I didn't want it to close; I'd fallen in love with that character. Some of the critics mentioned at the time what an interesting Williams I would make. Of course, the Nightingale was really Tennessee writing about himself. Except this was a more tragic character; an old, dying wino who had at one time been a promising artist.

So that's where the idea started. But I procrastinated, and I was still keeping my public relations job. A one-man show was the farthest thing from my mind. I was content that I'd had this success; I knew I could act again. I wanted it, but I wasn't ready to commit, giving up my job and going into it professionally. *Confessions of a Nightingale* was a fluke.

I call the show "an intimate visit" with Tennessee. It's all his words; I didn't make any of it up. He may not have said them in that context, but... it's all him. Charlotte Chandler did one of the last interviews with Tennessee before his death, and she had reams of material.

When I was working in public relations, we worked with Charlotte on her book, *The Ultimate Seduction*. Months later, when this show came up, I remembered her interview with Tennessee and reread it. That's how it started. Once New York became interested in the show, she got hot on it and started working with me. We had to lengthen it to 90 minutes. Originally we had some quotes from a *Playboy* interview; we took all that out for New York, due to contractual reasons, and strictly used Charlotte's material.

When I began putting the show together, someone loaned me a recording of Tennessee reading his poetry. I played the first band, and I stopped. I thought, if I start mimicking him, it's going to throw me as an actor; I'm just going to have to go with my own instincts and my own Southern dialect. Plus, if I copied Tennessee and used his cadence and everything, we'd still be at the theatre... he spoke *so* slow.

Williams every so often would lecture or do a question-and-answer session after a performance; he'd get up on stage and chat with the audience. So that was my premise. I wanted it as though he was just talking to the audience. And since it was designed as a tribute I didn't want to get into too much of the ugly side. I don't think a man talking to his audience would let all the warts hang out; I let enough of them hang out so that it's certainly indicative of some of his problems, without it being ugly.

I'd love to do a play sometime that goes into all of that. Shortly after he died, all those books started coming out which really told all the nitty gritty, and the really ugly side of things. I thought, there's enough negativity. But as an actor, I love all that; it's juicy stuff to play.

Some of the critics have said it's too nice a picture of Tennessee; well, that's one side of him. It wasn't designed to be the definitive story of his life. It's an introduction to the man, psychologically what made him tick, how he used his own self and own experiences in his characters. There's a little of Amanda from *Glass Menagerie* and little of a

Blanche from *Streetcar* in my Tennessee — I think those were definitely part of his personality. To me, Blanche DuBois has always been the greatest feminine role ever written, at least by an American playwright. I thought, why don't they ever write a role like that for an actor? Of course, now I'm getting to play a form of Blanche, in him.

People say, "Has Tennessee taken over your persona?" I don't think that at all. But this play has been very cathartic for me. It's almost been like, I wanted to do everything in reverse of Tennessee. He didn't want to get rid of his demons — he felt he'd lose his angels. If he went to a psychiatrist and stopped drinking, the drugs and the sex — those are the things that drove him. Whereas I wanted to get rid of any negativity in my life, as best I could. It's really a change of attitude...

The piece has been so rewarding; for young people who aren't that familiar with Williams, it serves as a good introduction. Shortly after I opened, a teacher at the University of Southern California asked me to do the show for his theatre class. They were all young kids. I don't think I got a single laugh, except when I mentioned anything about sex. That they understood. I've had so many people come backstage and say they've got to reread Williams' works. Not only is Tennessee keeping me alive, in a little way I'm reintroducing people to him. Other than being a working actor, that's the most rewarding thing.

I abhorred one-man shows. I'd seen John Gielgud and Emlyn Williams; Henry Fonda was a public relations client, so I saw his *Clarence Darrow*. But I've never seen Hal Holbrook or Julie Harris... I've seen very few. No matter how brilliant the actor is, in one-person shows I've never quite believed them, when they're in a play situation and they're pretending to talk to someone else — that there's another person there — they all seem like tricks to me. With mine, I wanted it so I was talking to the audience. That's a legitimate situation.

I think the greatest help for me [as an actor] was Alcoholics Anonymous. Hearing those stories the people tell at AA meetings, they'll go on for 60 minutes, 90 minutes — far more horrendous than Tennessee's stories — but if it's a good speaker, it's absolutely fascinating. If what you're saying is good, you don't have to move around, and dance a jig... for dramatic effect sometimes, it's certainly good to do that, but since I was trying to make it as honest as possible, I didn't want to move around unnecessarily.

I went to see Peggy Lee's one-woman show. She had had an accident and couldn't walk; she had to play the whole thing from a very fancy wheelchair. She's a marvelous singer — she really knows what to do with a lyric. She makes very few gestures. I'm not comparing myself to Peggy Lee — but watching her that night, I thought, "If you're commanding on the stage, you *can* sit for an hour, and talk or sing."

Now everybody wants to do a one-person show. I think I was just lucky; my timing was right. All of this good that's happened to me was a total shock and surprise. It was not premeditated at all. I was scared to death when I started doing it. But I thought, "What have you got to lose?" I didn't give up my job until this became successful and I knew I was going to New York.

I had the luxury of a year's run at the Beverly Hills Playhouse. That really was like a workshop. Each week I did it, I'd add a new paragraph. But I didn't do it all at once. Thank God I had that luxury of trying it out, putting things in, taking things out... With the new Equity Waiver rulings, shows can only run a certain length of time.

I'd like to eventually add a little music to it, then in a way I'm afraid to. The show is so successful, I'm afraid of anything that would take away from the honesty or its simplicity. I recently found some new material, some quotes — it's all good stuff but I haven't bothered to memorize it, and I don't know that I want to because of the length.

One critic said I reminded him of William Faulkner, and said I should play him. But at this point another one-man play is the farthest thing from my thoughts. I was talking to Julie Harris and she said, "Now you've got to get another one, so you can go back to all those places you've played." Maybe down the line, but I don't think so. The first one's quite enough.

The most difficult aspect is getting the energy up before you go up there each night. I can put things across even if I'm not feeling well... but some nights I think, "Oh, God, how am I going to go out there for 90 minutes?" I have to give myself a little lecture just before I go on... It's amazing once you're out there, your illnesses seem to disappear.

Playing this role, anything that's wrong with Ray Stricklyn, like a bad cold, I can incorporate into the part. One night I pulled a tendon in my leg in taking my bow; I could hardly walk offstage. The next two performances I used a cane. I was uncomfortable as Ray up there, but it worked. And I'm one of those old fools who believe the show must go on.

Life As Art

"I've been forbidden to describe this occasion as straight talk from a bent speaker. Let's call it a consultation with a doctor who is more ill than you are." Thus a mild-mannered, silver-haired Englishman set the tone for *An Evening with Quentin Crisp*, on a tour of America a decade ago.

The "self-confessed [and] self-evident homosexual" spoke openly about his unconventional lifestyle as he peppered the audience with shards of his off-the-wall philosophy, but said nothing for the sake of shock. "To do things to shock the neighbors is as absurd as to pander to them," he acknowledged.

The autobiographical monologue as a legitimate form of theatre had not quite emerged when the author of *The Naked Civil Servant* set out on tour with his one-man show, advising audiences how to rethink the world on one's own terms — as he had — and develop a personal style. Not until another charismatic individual appeared on the scene — a young actor who decided to rethink the theatre on his own terms — would the art form find widespread acceptance.

As careers in the theatre go, talking about one's self seems like a peculiar way to make a living — but Spalding Gray thrives on it. In the decade since Crisp traveled America, Gray has created and performed a dozen monologues based on his own life — and has become an influential cult figure in the process.

Gray himself was influenced not by other solo performers, but by novelists like Henry Miller, Jack Kerouac and
Thomas Wolfe, especially what he calls "Wolfe's confessional, discursive, associative ways of working, in novels
like *Look Homeward, Angel,* starting with one story, then
digressing… I was also influenced by Baba Ram Dass, his
early story-telling tapes, poets like Allen Ginsberg and
Robert Lowell, anyone working in the autobiographical
form."

As a college student, Gray fell into the habit of relating
the story of his day, at day's end, to an attentive group of
co-workers and fellow students. As a struggling actor living on the Lower East Side of Manhattan in the late sixties,
he "survived" on such stories. The words, however, "went
into deep hibernation" when Gray immersed himself in
New York's burgeoning underground theatre world, in
which he "rolled and grunted and screamed for 10 years."

The techniques he learned in Richard Schechner's ex-
perimental Performance Group deviated from his traditional acting background, in a way that unlocked his imagination. Schechner exerted a strong influence on the fledgling writer-performer with challenging exercises that taught
actors to be themselves before playing a role, and directions
to draw on their own needs rather than the character's.
Gray continued to explore himself and develop his own
idea of theatre in 1974, when he and three of his colleagues
broke off from Schechner to form what would become the
Wooster Group.

Under the direction of Elizabeth LeCompte, Gray and
his fellow actors collaborated on *Three Places in Rhode Island*
— a trilogy of autobiographical pieces that led directly to

the monologues he would later develop. *Rumstick Road*, the second work in the trilogy, was a docudrama about his mother's suicide, improvised around a series of audio tapes of his family members talking about the tragedy.

"Within that piece I would walk down and do direct address to the audience," he later recalled. "That's where I gave up the concept of character and began to make a character out of myself. I'd say, 'I'm Spalding Gray, and this is the house that I grew up in, in Barrington, Rhode Island.'"

Upon completion of the trilogy, he decided he had come to the end of the group collaborative process and began working solo. Beginning with his first monologue in 1979 — *Sex and Death to the Age of 14* — Gray performed from a outline rather than a script, tape-recording each performance and reworking the outline on a daily basis. The technique, which LeCompte and Gray used during rehearsals for the trilogy, gave the material a sense of freshness.

"What keeps the audience's attention is that they see I am grappling with the story, so it's very immediate. And I'm speaking it for the first time," says Gray, who uses the technique to this day. "What I'm grappling with is the memory. Trying to remember it, trying to get it as perfect as possible. So I'm rewriting it every night."

When Roland Joffe cast Gray in a small role as the American ambassador's aide in his film, *The Killing Fields* — set in Cambodia during the bloody aftermath of the Khmer Rouge occupation of Phnom Penh — the actor decided to keep a journal, knowing he would be "barraged with new experiences." Six months after the filming ended in Thailand he began to create a new monologue, in an

Spalding Gray in the screen version of *Swimming to Cambodia*, filmed at the Performing Garage in New York.

effort to help him readjust to "the terrific reverse culture shock" and segue from the "luxurious nonreality" of moviemaking to the monotony of everyday life.

Swimming to Cambodia evolved over a two-year period during 200 performances, premiering November 15, 1984 at the Performance Garage in lower Manhattan — the scene of his experiments with the Wooster Group. "In the beginning, I'm never sure what it is I'm talking about. I only begin to see the shape and meaning of a monologue after I have performed it a number of times... there are certain stories that through repeated telling, begin both to give me pleasure, and at the same time, to help me make sense of my life," says Gray.

"I am interested in what happens to the so-called facts after they have passed through performance and registered on my memory," ventures the 48-year-old solo performer, who likens himself to an impressionist painter or "poetic reporter." Instead of reporting at once, however, like a journalist, he does just the opposite: "I give the facts a chance to settle down until they blend, bubble and mix in the swamp of dream, memory and reflection." He admits to embellishing the truth a bit but does not fictionalize events.

Unlike his earlier monologues, *Cambodia* was a mix of personal experience and outside research. To his rambling meditation on the bizarre odyssey of making the film — the shooting of a scene that required 66 takes, the cast's off-camera recreation in massage parlors, and his search for the "organic perfect moment" once the filming was over — Gray added the political history, discussing American bombing strategy in Indochina and the rise of the Khmer Rouge.

The two-part three-hour monologue has found a second life — and a far wider audience — as a 87-minute film, which Gray has jokingly described as *My Dinner with Andre* without the dinner or Andre. "It is not that elaborate," as film critic John Stackpole observed, despite the inclusion of film clips from *The Killing Fields*. "But it adds up to more than a sit-down comic routine. The bitter wisdom and artful precision hint at what it must have been like to listen at the feet of Homer."

Gray, who has been compared to everyone from Mark Twain to Woody Allen — to his displeasure — has a decided preference for "mining my own psychic landscapes" when it comes to performing. But not exclusively. "I'm not interested in being stuck in one bag. I miss ensemble work enormously," he says, explaining his appearance as the Stage Manager in a recent production of *Our Town*. Since etching *Cambodia* on celluloid, he has also been seen in a number of films — including *Clara's Heart*, as a grief counselor, and *Beaches*, as a doctor.

His latest autobiographical odyssey is a book, tentatively titled *Impossible Vacations*. In 1988 he performed a selection from the work-in-progress as a monologue in Los Angeles, "testing it out in an oral way." In the course of the evening, he took the audience from Australia to Bali to Las Vegas to New England — and ultimately explored his mother's insanity and suicide, retracing the intimate territory of the *Rhode Island* trilogy that gave birth to his unusual career as a solo performer.

What motivates an admittedly private person to reveal the most intimate details of his life to the public? "I'm not sure. It's one of the idiosyncratic parts of my nature," Gray said in a recent interview. "It's an enormous challenge to take what's private and go public with it... I'd rather speak in front of a group of people than be at a party; it has more meaning for me."

Gray has had wide influence on writers, performers and other theatre practitioners. Los Angeles-based director Mark W. Travis, who witnessed *Cambodia* in its stage incarnation, has since functioned as midwife for three successful one-man shows of an autobiographical nature. "The first time I saw Spalding I was mesmerized by him," recalls Travis. "He brought total revelation of himself to the audience, unabashedly presenting his strengths and weaknesses and reflecting upon his own life in a very unique way... a different form of theatre I had never even considered or been aware of."

Travis, who got his start at the Yale School of Drama in the mid-sixties, directed dozens of productions before venturing into the form Gray introduced to him. The concept for the first of his three solo shows was born in a highly unlikely setting — at a memorial service for the wife of actor-friend Paul Linke, whom he had directed in a two-character improvisational piece.

Linke's eulogy for his wife Francesca — who died of cancer at 37 — became the seed for a remarkable monologue. "The idea was really generated by his ability to sort of pull that whole audience together, and move them out of that somber, mournful mood, from a sense of loss to a sense of celebration," says Travis, who suggested Linke do a one-man show instead of the multi-character play about death and dying he had already contemplated.

The actor wasn't sure what Travis meant until he saw *Swimming to Cambodia* — "that was when I realized one guy can be entertaining," notes Linke. Actor and director met periodically for lunch, and Linke told Travis stories about

Paul Linke's solo, *Times Flies When You're Alive,* is far too
intimate for some theatregoers.

his wife's battle with breast cancer, and their fruitless attempts to find a holistic alternative to chemotherapy.

Linke, who supplied comic relief on TV's *CHiPs* for six seasons, has two decades of theatre work to his credit, including a stint as master of ceremonies at the Garden Theatre Festival in Los Angeles. "I used to emcee all the acts, so I did have a lot of experience standing in front of an audience with nothing, no material — just my presence, just me," he observes. "The one thing I think I really developed there which I'm able to use is the ability to look at the audience like a friendly mass. I try to make it like they're in my home — connect with them, talk to them."

He first got a sense of the show when he performed a 10-minute segment at a benefit. "I don't remember how people reacted," says Linke. "The woman who was hosting the evening said, 'How about a warm hand for a brave man?' and I was out in the night air; I didn't know what to think. This lawyer I'd met earlier came outside. He lit a cigarette, he started talking about how nice the night was, how wonderful the garden looked... finally he said, 'My best friend died 12 years ago, and I realize now I never dealt with it.' Right then I knew: 'That's what this show is about.'"

Time Flies When You're Alive opened in 1987 at the 99-seat Powerhouse Theatre in Santa Monica, California. The actor has no recollection of the first night, apart from walking onstage and walking off — and the feeling that "it was important to tell these things, because I wanted to bring death out of the closet." Like Spalding Gray, he had a story to tell, but no script.

While Travis helped Linke put together a structure for the show, the actor had to experiment with the content to find out what would work. "For a while I thought of using props — I found a jar of tumors that Francesca had pulled out of her chest and I thought, I'm going to use this. And I did, in one performance," reports Linke. "At one point I looked at the audience and I said, 'Have you ever seen cancer?' And I pulled them out of the box and went down to the front row... and people were going, 'Oh, God...' So I dropped the tumors. I had a thing called tumor humor, which I also dropped."

There is a lot of unexpected humor in the show. "Like life," says the 40-year-old actor. Like the moment when his three children are helping him spread his wife's ashes in the California mountains and he tells his youngest son, "You got your mother all over your shoes."

The most poignant moment in the program is the scene in which he recreates his wife's death at home. He talks about a beautiful light in the room that day and manages to bring that light into the theatre as he comforts her, telling her to "relax... relax... relax... go with God..." as he finally lets go himself. When the tears stream down his face, he is not acting. "I've done it over 100 times and I think I've only not wept twice. I'm reliving it, sometimes I'm right there," confides Linke. "I don't feel obligated to cry, but... the emotion is there. The tears are real."

If the intimacy of the subject matter seems ideally suited to the intimacy of the solo approach, it is far too intimate for some. "There's no escape, unless you just walk out — as some people do," concedes the actor. "At first when it happened, I took it very personally. Then after a while I realized the reason they were leaving was because they couldn't handle it, it was too intense. Then I felt better."

Linke and Travis have had difficulty in determining

how best to present *Time Flies,* or describe it. "Whenever you tell someone, 'Well, it's a one-man show about a guy talking about his wife who died of cancer,' they go, 'Give me a break. I really don't want to go see that.' But it's not a downer," maintains Linke. "It's an uplifting, positive thing."

Los Angeles Times theatre critic Sylvie Drake agreed: "It is a shattering picture of one fragile family's terrifying voyage through upheaval and trauma... as well as a husband and father's growing affirmation and strength in coping with loss. In no small way, it is also a stunning affirmation of life." Spalding Gray has called it "the most vivid and intense solo theatre I have ever seen... a fine balance between a life lived and a life reflected upon."

The show, which ran for a year at the Tiffany Theatre in Los Angeles, has since gone on tour, and has been filmed for broadcast on Home Box Office. "I really had no expectations. I expected to do maybe six performances, 20-30 people would come each night, and hopefully it wouldn't be too embarrassing," says Linke, who credits much of the success of *Time Flies When You're Alive* to Mark Travis' efforts: "He wore many hats lumped together under the title of producer-director."

Why has the show enjoyed such success? "I think it makes people feel; it taps into their hearts. It's something people recognize and respond to. I think also there's a lot of need in our society to talk about death," asserts Linke. "People are pretty free to discuss their sexuality today... but when you come to death, it's still deep in the closet."

The topic of Travis' second solo production is another subject deep in the closet: child abuse. Like its predecessor, *No Place Like Home* is a story told by the man who lived it —

survived it — a story of almost unimaginable physical abuse and psychological horror experienced by actor Shane McCabe.

When McCabe presented a piece of his tortured past as a monologue in an acting class, it was so well received he decided to develop it as an audition piece. About that time, he went to see *Time Flies* with a friend. "When I realized there was a viable place for a one-man show with this kind of material," recalls McCabe, "I turned to my friend and I said, 'Within a year, I'm going to get that director, and I'm going to do a one-man show in this theatre.'"

Months later, McCabe performed one of his autobiographical monologues at an acting workshop conducted by Travis. They began to develop the show piece by piece in class, with McCabe bringing in chapters as weekly assignments — a painful task for the 48-year-old former accountant, who has been a professional actor for the past 10 years.

"I had a lot of second thoughts about ever doing this. It became so personal at times I couldn't go on," he confides. "I had been in therapy for years, and I had told my therapist a lot. Then I had opened myself up to Mark as a friend and director, and told him the stories; but I had never told anyone else. To present this for the class was the first time I was baring my soul to the public."

Going public with private information was a problem Travis encountered with both McCabe and Linke. "Sometimes I would discover some material they couldn't handle talking about; even though they wanted to really expose everything and they wanted to deal with everything, there were elements they didn't want to put out. But it's not an easy road out there for either of these guys," acknowledges Travis, who observes, "You become more than just a direc-

Shane McCabe reveals the horrors of his childhood in *No Place Like Home.*

tor. You become a father confessor, a psychologist, you hold their hand…"

No Place Like Home, which opened at Los Angeles' Tiffany Theatre in 1988, is more than a litany of bruises and broken bones. McCabe's "journey through childhood" is ultimately a triumph of the human spirit, the story of a boy who survived physical and mental torture by recreating old movies in his closet — where he was virtually imprisoned for seven years — and choreographing dance routines in his head.

It is a tale of survival McCabe feels people need to hear: "I'll have someone come up to me after the show and say, 'I was an abused child.' And I know this is the first time this person has ever told a stranger that." Such revelations are "the healthiest thing that can happen. Child abuse is kind of a taboo subject and we're just now starting to talk about it. People need to know that they can talk about this," affirms the actor, who hopes his show will enable him to raise money for child abuse centers and bring an awareness to the general public.

McCabe's show is "the riskiest" of Travis' much-heralded solo presentations, feels the director — "there are a lot of people he doesn't ever want to know that he's doing it." His most commercial one-man show, he feels, is the third and most recent, *A Bronx Tale* — which developed much like McCabe's, from an acting class monologue.

Chazz Palminteri's story, in which he plays all the characters of the tough neighborhood he grew up in during the sixties, chronicles his education in "the school of the street" in graphic detail. The show opened early in 1989 to high praise; one critic called it "world class theatre."

Travis blames his success on Spalding Gray. "If it hadn't been for Spalding, I probably never would have gotten into any of this," he contends. Despite the rave reviews his work has garnered, Travis concedes that such shows can be hard to sell — and their subject matter is not the only problem.

"Just because it's a one-man show some people think it's not going to be very interesting," explains the award-winning director, who admits that he himself had never been enamored of the solo form. "The character is usually in a false situation. You've got Freud talking to an audience of 200 people in a theatre for two hours. Why is he doing that? Julie Harris is brilliant, but I still ask myself, who is she talking to? She's not talking to me," says Travis.

"Hal Holbrook as Mark Twain works, because Twain himself was a storyteller. Paul, Shane and Chazz are all highly talented storytellers; their shows are all done in that vein. The thing I find intriguing with these shows is that we immediately break the fourth wall and recognize the fact that we're in a theatre. There's no artifice.

"There are some critics who have said, 'Is it theatre?'" muses Travis. "Other critics have said, 'This should not be in a theatre, and we should not be subjected to it.' It seems to me they have a very limited view of what theatre is." Paul Linke, whose show has been the target of more than one such review, concurs. "I think about the success *Time Flies* has had, and I laugh," he says. "If it isn't theatre, whatever it is, it works. And I think it works because it really moves people."

"I get angry when critics say things like, 'This isn't theatre, this is therapy,'" declares Shane McCabe. "They have no idea who I am as a person, whether this is therapy or catharsis for me or not... no one in the audience has ever said, 'This is wonderful therapy.' I get comment sheets back saying: 'This is fascinating theatre... This is not art as life, this is life as art.'"

The autobiographical monologue now in vogue is not a modern invention, notes Travis. "Someone said to me once, 'You're breaking new ground... you're creating a new theatrical form here.' I said, 'That's not true at all.' What we're really doing is going back to a very primitive form of theatre, the genesis of theatre. Theatre started with someone saying to a group of people, 'I'm going to tell you a story.'

"We're also going back to — and this is what I find exciting — the power of the actor, to create just with words, and with his ability as an actor. He can take you anywhere in the world. This is really the essence of theatre — the power of the actor to stimulate the imagination of an audience. And to pull an audience into a very personal odyssey." Real or fabricated the process is the same, contends Travis, whose primary task is to edit the presentation into a cohesive whole, much like a documentary film.

"People who say this is not theatre, or this doesn't belong in a theatre, feel so threatened by what we're doing that I get concerned for them. I don't know why it makes them so uneasy," says the director.

"One aspect of these shows that can't be denied, is that in many ways it's highly confrontational. The actor recognizes that you're there and he talks to you; he's going to include you and he's not going to put up a fourth wall. A lot of people can't handle it. They say, 'This isn't theatre, it doesn't belong here, don't do this to me.' They're doing it to themselves," reasons the director, who feels theatregoers should look inward if they have trouble dealing with the intimate subject matter of his solo shows. "Theatre needs to push out at the edges," asserts Travis.

"The theatre should be a place where you know you're going to go in and be challenged. It doesn't always have to be a place of comfort and sheer entertainment."

Epilogue

Four years ago, I fell in love with a remarkable woman. It was one of those whirlwind romances, the kind you never forget. The affair continues to this day — and my wife isn't the least bit jealous. The other woman is the late Edna St. Vincent Millay, the Pulitzer Prize-winning poet, humanist and social conscience who was 50 years ahead of her time. The affair began when I was asked to help create a play, in which she had been cast as the sole character.

I am not the first one to fall in love with the poet. Bettye Ackerman, an actress and friend of long acquaintance, who co-starred in the *Ben Casey* TV series some years ago, has had a great passion for Millay for many years. Bettye has given readings of the poetry, but what she wants to do is *play* Millay — to put her on stage in a one-woman play, as her friend Pat Carroll did with Gertrude Stein.

Edna St. Vincent Millay. The name is certainly familiar, but I know nothing about her when Bettye asks me to collaborate on the script in the fall of 1985. I am noncommittal, until she loans me a collection of Millay's letters. As soon as I read them, I see the potential — and the challenge.

I have a lot of catching up to do. I read Millay's *Collected Poems* and several biographies. But *The Letters of Edna St. Vincent Millay* are the primary source of information; they offer tremendous insight into her personality, her relationship with her mother, her love life and her outlook on the human condition. I also study the craft of writing a one-woman play, by reading and analyzing William Luce's *The Belle of Amherst* and Marty Martin's *Gertrude Stein Gertrude Stein Gertrude Stein*.

Bettye knows Millay's life and work intimately. She has hundreds of notes and ideas. She doesn't know where to begin. We talk concept, format, style. We decide the play should take place on the last night of Millay's life, in the poetry room of her house at Steepletop near Austerlitz, New York. We agree that she should not speak to imaginary characters; we will simply put Millay on the stage and let her talk directly to the audience.

How will we begin the play? With one of Millay's poems? Perhaps "First Fig," the one poem everyone seems to know and love, about "burning the candle at both ends" — no, God no. It is so well known, it is to be excluded altogether. To hold an audience for 90 minutes, with a single actor on stage, we will have to surprise them; avoid the obvious, the familiar, the expected at every turn.

Our play will not be the first attempt to put Millay on stage. Dorothy Stickney assembled and performed a solo recital made up of poems and letters in 1960. But it dealt with only the niceties. Bettye makes it clear she wants to deal with all sides of Millay's personality — her overt sexuality, her obsession with death, her self-destructive behavior.

Bettye feels the theme should be that Millay put her work before everything else. From the beginning, she identifies strongly with Millay. When I add the line to the script,

"Whatever I do, I give my whole self to it" — Bettye thinks I am quoting *her*. It is direct from Millay. She also identifies with Pat Carroll. Bettye has taken a tremendous burden on her shoulders, as the cast of one in this full-length play about her favorite poet, and she now knows exactly what Pat meant when she said — in preparation for *Gertrude Stein* — "I wanted to commit suicide at least three times."

Bettye will be alone on stage, but she'll have an ally in Ted Post, a longtime friend with over 40 years of directing experience in theatre, TV and films. Ted agrees to join the project while we are working on the rough draft. The first day we meet, he questions the use of a word on page one of the script. Then he launches into a discussion of language, the type of words you use in theatre vs. literature. I know immediately that Bettye has made the right choice of director.

By the time I finish the second draft with Ted and Bettye in 1987, the script has been completely rewritten. It isn't simply a matter of dramatizing Millay's letters, but of getting inside her head and filling in the missing pieces of the puzzle that was her life. There are a great many things neither Millay nor her biographers touched on; we have to create them, based on what we know. Millay has left emotional fingerprints all over her letters, and Ted pounces on them, with the tenacity of a bulldog and the skill of a forensics expert.

"Why does Millay say that? Why does she feel that way? Probe into her insides," challenges Ted. "What did she experience? To what avail, to what end? Analyze what the character is thinking. Justify it — why does she do what she does?"

Ted will ultimately give the play a depth and a dimension it would not have without him. I resist many of his suggestions to begin with, but he defends everything passionately and wins me over in almost every instance. He is not a writer, by his own admission, but he is a terrific catalyst for me, and a great teacher.

Early in 1989, after many delays, we are ready to go into rehearsals. We are given free rehearsal space at Temple Beth Am in Los Angeles. In exchange, we offer to do a benefit. Ted arranges a six-week schedule to "allow us time to osmose, to digest — otherwise you skim over problems." With the generous patience of the temple, rehearsal will continue for four months.

Ted begins by telling Bettye to "go with your instincts" when she runs through the scene, instead of suggesting moves to her. Forget the lines, he says, go with the instincts. Otherwise the performance will be too intellectual. "Find the reason first — the words will come. Trust the instinct to follow through on the thought."

Early on, we discuss a few of the solo shows we've seen over the years; ultimately, they give us more ideas about what we *don't* want to do, rather than things we might do. Ted tells Bettye he wants constant movement. He doesn't want her to sit or stand at any point and simply recite text, as many solo performers do. He equates stationary with static; he rarely allows Bettye to stop talking or moving.

In the first week of rehearsal, Ted wonders aloud: "How

can I extract as much emotional involvement from the material as possible?" That's the glue that is going to hold this play together, he insists — the thing that will cement the words in Bettye's memory without a supporting cast to fall back on, the thing that will keep an audience tuned in to a singular voice. "That's what theatre's all about," he says. "Convert everything into an emotional experience."

By the second week, Ted is giving Bettye a rigorous workout, the likes of which she hasn't had in years. Ted is stretching her acting muscles and really pushing her hard. She is wholly open to his direction — whatever he says, she does. Her reading of the dramatic scenes is strong at the outset. The lighter material is much more difficult. But there is no one else to supply the comic relief; she will have to be both comedian and tragedian.

Ted's interpretation of a major scene changes almost week by week, necessitating constant script revisions. I comply on the spot. When the lines don't work with the emotional underpinning he extracts from the scene, the lines have to change — not the direction.

The transitions are the toughest. Rewrite. Rewrite. Rewrite. I begin to wonder if they will ever work. Bettye reminds us of the adage that it takes two people to make a great painting: one to paint it, one to tell the painter when to stop. Even as we near the end of four months rehearsal, Ted is coming up with changes. When Bettye objects, he insists, "Art is a living force."

Talk about the theatre, making things work — making this thing work — continues during lunch. In the parking lot after a day's rehearsal, there is still more conversation. There is no refuge from the discussion — even in the men's room.

Ted has never directed a one-person play before. Yet he jumps into it as though he's been doing it all his life. What he has been doing all his life is theatre. And that's what we're doing — but it is highly intensified theatre, because everything has to be communicated by one person. He tells Bettye to take an intimate, conversational approach. "You can't talk to 3,000 people — talk to one."

This confirms what Bettye already knows. She has to take the audience in as her confidant, sharing the intimate moments of a life with them. "I always thought of this as a confessional — the audience is my best friend," she says, during a break in rehearsal. Later, she recalls having seen one of Ruth Draper's solo performances: "I just loved her... never dreaming that I would do such a thing."

I had often dreamt that I would do such a thing as write a play and get it "on the boards." Fifteen days into rehearsal, I have ambivalent feelings about the project. The play has taken over my life — everything else is going to hell. It is a truth Bettye and Ted both know, and I have to discover for myself. Still, it is one of the great experiences of my life.

"You're working on a one-woman show?" says an acquaintance. "That must be the hardest thing to do, to keep people interested for an hour and a half." A visitor to rehearsal at Temple Beth Am, on learning it is my first play, says cheerfully, "This is like a baptism of fire for you." "Yes," I reply. "And it's the first baptism that's ever taken place in a synagogue."

Appendix

A selection of one-person shows discussed in this book, indicating first performance, New York debut, radio, television or film production, availability of record, audio or video cassette, and script. Except where noted, the performer served as his own uncredited director.

AGES OF MAN

Adapted by John Gielgud from George Ryland's Shakespeare anthology, *The Ages of Man*. Performed by Gielgud. First public performance: September 1957, Edinburgh Festival. New York debut: December 28, 1958, 46th Street Theatre. London debut: July 8, 1959, Queen's Theatre. TV: January 23, 1966, CBS; October 2, 1966, BBC. Film: Time/Life. Record, audio: Caedmon.

BEGINNING TO END

Selected and arranged by Jack MacGowran from the works of Samuel Beckett. Performed by MacGowran. Original title: *End of Day*. U.S. title: *Jack MacGowran in the Works of Samuel Beckett*. First performance: October 5, 1962, Gaiety Theatre, Dublin; directed by Donald McWhinnie. TV: February 23, 1965, BBC; directed by Patrick Garland. Record: Claddagh. Revised production: Théâtre Édouard VII, Paris, April 23, 1970; directed by Beckett (uncredited). New York debut: November 19, 1970, Public Theater. TV: November 4, 1971, KCET. Script: Gotham Book Mart.

THE BELLE OF AMHERST

Written by William Luce, based on the life and work of Emily Dickinson. Performed by Julie Harris. Directed by Charles Nelson Reilly. First performance: February 25, 1976, Moore Egyptian Theatre, Seattle. New York debut: April 28, 1976, Longacre Theater. TV: December 29, 1976, KCET. Record: Credo. Video: International Film Exchange. Script: Houghton Mifflin.

BRIEF LIVES
Adapted by Patrick Garland from the works of John Aubrey. Performed by Roy Dotrice. Directed by Garland. First performance: January 16, 1967, Hampstead Theatre Club, London. New York debut: December 18, 1967, John Golden Theatre. TV: May 6, 1968, BBC. Record: Major Minor. Script: Faber & Faber.

BRONTË
Written by William Luce, based on the life and work of Charlotte Brontë. Performed by Julie Harris. Original title: *Currer Bell, Esq.* First production: October 14, 1982, WGBH Radio; directed by Elinor Stout. Film for TV: December 4, 1982, Telefís Éireann; directed by Delbert Mann. First stage performance: November 7, 1983, L.A. Stage Company West, Los Angeles; directed by Kristoffer Tabori. Record, audio: Caedmon. Revised production: September 29, 1985, Beverly Hills Theatre Guild, Beverly Hills, Calif.; directed by Charles Nelson Reilly. Script: Samuel French.

CONFESSIONS OF A NIGHTINGALE
Adapted by Charlotte Chandler and Ray Stricklyn from Chandler's *The Ultimate Seduction.* Performed by Stricklyn. First performance: January 4, 1985, Beverly Hills Playhouse, Beverly Hills, Calif. New York debut: September 23, 1986, Audrey Wood Playhouse; directed by John Tillinger. Script: Samuel French.

CONFESSIONS OF AN IRISH REBEL
Written and adapted by Shay Duffin, from the works of Brendan Behan. Performed by Duffin. Directed by Denis Hayes. Original title: *Shay Duffin as Brendan Behan.* First performance: September 1971, Gigi's Disco, Quebec. First public performance: January 2, 1972, Theatre in the Dell, Toronto. New York debut: January 2, 1973, Abbey Theatre. TV: 1983, Group W. Record: Potato.

EMLYN WILLIAMS AS CHARLES DICKENS
Selected and arranged by Emlyn Williams from the works of Dickens. Performed by Williams. First performance: July 1951, Old Vic School, Dulwich. London debut: October 29, 1951, Lyric Theatre, Hammersmith. New York debut: February 4, 1952, John

Golden Theater. TV: December 30, 1951, BBC; January 29, 1967, CBS. Radio: August 19, 1952, BBC. Record: Argo.

GERTRUDE STEIN GERTRUDE STEIN GERTRUDE STEIN
Written by Marty Martin. Performed by Pat Carroll. Directed by Milton Moss. First public performance: May 4, 1979, Penn State, University Park, Pa. New York debut: June 6, 1979, Circle Repertory Theater. TV: February 13, 1982, CBS Cable. Record, audio: Caedmon. Script: Random House/Vintage.

HERE ARE LADIES
Selected and arranged by Siobhán McKenna from the works of Irish writers. Performed by McKenna. Directed by Sean Kenny. First performance: 1970, Oxford Playhouse, Oxford. London debut: July 28, 1970, Criterion Theatre. New York debut: February 22, 1971, Public Theatre. TV: Telefís Éireann.

I'LL GO ON
Adapted by Gerry Dukes and Barry McGovern from Samuel Beckett's trilogy, *Molloy, Malone Dies* and *The Unnamable*. Performed by McGovern. Directed by Colm O Briain. First performance: September 23, 1985, Gate Theatre, Dublin. New York debut: June 22, 1988, Mitzi Newhouse Theater.

IAN McKELLEN ACTING SHAKESPEARE
Selected and arranged by Ian McKellen from the works of Shakespeare. Performed by McKellen. Original title: *Acting Shakespeare.* First performance: September 1976, Edinburgh Festival. New York debut: April 1981. Official New York debut: January 19, 1984, Ritz Theatre. TV: April 1982, PBS.

THE IMPORTANCE OF BEING OSCAR
Selected and arranged by Micheál Mac Liammóir from the works of Oscar Wilde. Performed by Mac Liammóir. Directed by Hilton Edwards. First production: September 19, 1960, Gaiety Theatre, Dublin. London debut: October 1960, Apollo Theatre. New York debut: March 14, 1961, Lyceum Theatre. Radio: July 25, 1963, BBC. Record: Columbia. Script: Dolmen Press (out of print).

JAMES JOYCE'S WOMEN

Written and adapted by Fionnula Flanagan from the works of Joyce. Performed by Flanagan. Directed by Burgess Meredith. First performance: August 25, 1977, South Coast Repertory Theatre, Costa Mesa, Calif. Film: 1985, Universal; directed by Michael Pearce. Video: MCA.

THE LAST FLAPPER

Written by William Luce, based on the writings of Mrs. F. Scott Fitzgerald. Original title: *Zelda.* First performance: May 31, 1980, Piccolo Spoleto Festival, Charleston, S.C.; performed by Lane Yorke, directed by Milton Moss. New York debut: October 23, 1984, American Place Theatre; performed by Olga Bellin, directed by Paul Roebling. Revised production: December 14, 1986, Burt Reynolds Theatre, Jupiter, Fla.; performed by Piper Laurie, directed by Charles Nelson Reilly. Script: Samuel French.

LILLIAN

Written by William Luce, based on the works of Lillian Hellman. Performed by Zoe Caldwell. Directed by Robert Whitehead. First performance: October 11, 1985, Cleveland Play House. New York debut: January 16, 1986, Ethel Barrymore Theatre. Script: Dramatists Play Service.

MARK TWAIN TONIGHT!

Selected and arranged by Hal Holbrook from the works of Twain. Performed by Holbrook. First performance: March 19, 1954, State Teachers College, Lockhaven, Pa. New York debut: April 6, 1959, 41st Street Theatre. TV: March 1967, CBS. Record: Columbia. Audio: CBS. Script: Ives Washburn (out of print).

NO PLACE LIKE HOME

Written and performed by Shane McCabe. Directed by Mark W. Travis. First performance: October 12, 1988, Tiffany Theater, Los Angeles.

ST. MARK'S GOSPEL

Conceived and performed by Alec McCowen. First performance: December 13, 1977, University Theatre, Newcastle. London debut: January 8, 1978, Riverside Studios, Hammersmith. New York debut: September 7, 1978, Marymount Manhattan Theatre. Radio: December 31, 1978, BBC.

THE SEARCH FOR SIGNS OF INTELLIGENT LIFE
IN THE UNIVERSE

Written by Jane Wagner. Performed by Lily Tomlin. Directed by Wagner. First performance: January 1985. New York debut: September 26, 1985, Plymouth Theater. Script: Harper & Row.

SECRET HONOR: THE LAST TESTAMENT OF
RICHARD M. NIXON

Written by Donald Freed and Arnold M. Stone. Performed by Philip Baker Hall. Directed by Robert Harders. First performance: June 1983, Los Angeles Actor's Theatre. New York debut: September 1983, Provincetown Playhouse. Film: 1984, Cinecom Pictures; directed by Robert Altman. Video: Vestron. Script: *New Plays USA 2*, Theatre Communications Group.

STUFF AS DREAMS ARE MADE ON

Adapted by Fred Curchack from *The Tempest* by William Shakespeare. Performed by Curchack. First performance: September 1983, Cinnabar Theatre, Petaluma, Calif.

SWIMMING TO CAMBODIA

Written and performed by Spalding Gray. First performance: November 15, 1984, Performing Garage, New York. Film: 1987, Cinecom Pictures; directed by Jonathan Demme. Video: Warner. Script: Theatre Communications Group.

TIME FLIES WHEN YOU'RE ALIVE

Written and performed by Paul Linke. Directed by Mark W. Travis. First performance: October 14, 1987, Powerhouse Theater, Santa Monica, Calif. New York debut: April 30, 1988, Playwrights

Horizons Theater. Film for TV: 1989, HBO; directed by Roger Spottiswoode.

VENUS AND ADONIS
Written by William Shakespeare. Performed by Benjamin Stewart. First performance: January 8, 1984, Itchey Foot Ristorante, Los Angeles.

WILL ROGERS' U.S.A.
Adapted by Paul Shyre from the works of Will Rogers. Performed by James Whitmore. Directed by Shyre. First official performance: January 12, 1970, Greenville Community Theatre, Greenville, S.C. New York debut: May 6, 1974, Helen Hayes Theatre. TV: 1972, CBS. Record: Columbia. Audio: Newman.

A WOMAN OF INDEPENDENT MEANS
Adapted by Elizabeth Forsythe Hailey from her novel. Performed by Barbara Rush. Directed by Normen Cohen. First performance: January 1984, Back Alley Theatre, Van Nuys, Calif. New York debut: May 3, 1984, Biltmore Theatre.

Selected Bibliography

PROLOGUE

Baker, Henry Barton, *English Actors*, New York: Henry Holt, 1879.

Highfill, Philip H. Jr., et al. *A Biographical Dictionary of Actors, Actresses, Musicians, Dancers, Managers and Other Stage Personnel in London, 1660-1800*, Carbondale: Southern Illinois University Press, 1973-.

Hume, Robert D., ed. *The London Theatre World, 1660-1800.* Carbondale: Southern Illinois University Press, 1980.

Kahan, Gerald. *George Alexander Stevens and The Lecture on Heads*, Athens: The University of Georgia Press, 1984.

Klepac, Richard L. *Mr. Mathews at Home*, London: Society for Theatre Research, 1979.

THE ART OF ACTING SOLO

Arkatov, Janice. "Not-So-Shy Side of David Cale Is Entertaining at the Taper, Too," *The Los Angeles Times*, February 13, 1988.

_____. "Reacquainting the World With the Paul Robeson Story," *The Los Angeles Times*, November 3, 1988.

Drake, Sylvie. "Barbara Rush: Solo Flight With *Independent Means*," *The Los Angeles Times*, March 28, 1984.

Klein, Alvin. "War Heroine's Role is Actress's Mission," *The New York Times*, June 9, 1985.

Krutch, Joseph Wood. "Drama," *The Nation*, February 23, 1952.

Lindfors, Viveca. *Viveka...Viveca*, New York: Everest House, 1981.

McCowen, Alec. *Double Bill*, New York: Atheneum, 1980.

Smith, Mark Chalon. "*A Woman* Takes the Stage Solo," *The Los Angeles Times*, November 13, 1987.

Young, Jordan. Interview with Scott Alsop, May 2, 1989.

_____. Interview with Carroll O'Connor, January 28, 1975.

THE QUEEN AND HER DISCIPLES

Drutman, Irving. "'Dear Ladies: Goodbye Forever, Cornelia,'" *The New York Times*, April 24, 1966.

Fein, Esther B. "Lily Tomlin: Comedy With Bite," *The New York Times,* September 22, 1985.

Grenfell, Joyce. *Joyce Grenfell Requests the Pleasure,* New York: St. Martin's Press, 1976.

McKenna, Muriel. "The Art of Ruth Draper," in Helen Chinoy and Linda Jenkins, ed. *Women in American Theatre,* New York: Crown, 1981.

Taylor, Clarke. "Tomlin's Comet, Wagner's Saga," *The Los Angeles Times,* October 7, 1985.

Warren, Neilla, ed. *The Letters of Ruth Draper,* New York: Scribner's, 1979.

Zabel, Morton D. *The Art of Ruth Draper,* New York: Doubleday, 1960.

IN PERSON

Arkatov, Janice. "One-Woman Show Reveals Human Side of Joan of Arc," *The Los Angeles Times,* January 8, 1988.

_____. "'Lovability' Plays No Part in Hall's Roles," *The Los Angeles Times,* August 1, 1988.

Berkvist, Robert. "'About All I Do Is Cut My Hair Differently,'" *The New York Times,* October 30, 1977.

Christon, Lawrence. "Bullish on T.R. as a Solo Act," *The Los Angeles Times,* June 5, 1977.

Findlater, Richard. *Emlyn Williams,* London: Rockliff, 1956.

Rintels, David W. *Clarence Darrow,* New York: Samuel French, 1975.

Smith, Cecil. "Abe Lincoln With a Stiff Upper Lip," *The Los Angeles Times,* February 7, 1981.

Sullivan, Dan. "One is Not the Loneliest Number," *The Los Angeles Times,* October 12, 1975.

Viertel, Jack. "Acting like the (Charles) Dickens," *The Los Angeles Herald Examiner,* January 24, 1982.

WILL THE REAL MARK TWAIN PLEASE STAND UP?

Christon, Lawrence. "Hal Holbrook's Twain Talks to 20th Century," *The Los Angeles Times,* May 30, 1985.

Goldman, William. *The Season: A Candid Look at Broadway,* New York: Harcourt, Brace & World, 1969.

Holbrook, Hal. *Mark Twain Tonight! An Actor's Portrait,* New York: Ives Washburn, 1959.

_____. "Twain chided with a chuckle," *Boston Sunday Globe,* March 5, 1972.

_____. Letter to the author, June 16, 1989.

Millstein, Gilbert. "One as Twain," *The New York Times Magazine,* April 19, 1959.

Young, Jordan R. *Let Me Entertain You: Conversations With Show People,* Beverly Hills: Moonstone Press, 1988.

_____. Interview with Bill McLinn, October 6, 1987.

_____. Interview with Ray Reinhardt, April 29, 1988.

HOMAGE TO THE BARD

Brandreth, Gyles. *John Gielgud: A Celebration,* Boston: Little, Brown and Company, 1984.

Butler, Patrick. "Tempest is brewing in his novel *Dream,*" *Chicago Skyline,* March 3, 1988.

Farber, Stephen. "Enter McKellen, Bearing Shakespeare," *The New York Times,* January 15, 1984.

Funke, Lewis and Booth, John E. *Actors Talk About Acting,* New York: Random House, 1961.

Gielgud, John. *An Actor and His Time,* London: Sidgwick and Jackson, 1979.

_____. Letter to the author, January 10, 1989.

Guidry, Frederick H. "McKellen's living scrapbook on Shakespeare," *The Christian Science Monitor,* September 18, 1987.

Harwood, Ronald, ed. *The Ages of Gielgud: An Actor at Eighty,* London: Hodder and Stoughton, 1984.

Herman, Jan. "Dramatization of *Venus* to Honor Bard," *The Los Angeles Times,* June 21, 1988.

Millstein, Gilbert. "Applause for a King," *The New York Times,* January 4, 1959.

Saville, Jonathan. "The McKellen Act," *The Reader,* San Diego, Calif., October 15, 1987.

Valeo, Tom. "Interpretation of *Tempest* reveals magic of stagecraft," *Daily Herald,* Chicago, March 14, 1988.

Young, Jordan R. Interview with Fred Curchack, April 12, 1989.

MONOLOGUE: PAT CARROLL

Carroll, Pat. "Re-Creating Stein in Paris," *Horizon*, November 1980.

Galligan, David. "Pat Carroll Pat Carroll Pat Carroll," *Drama-Logue*, January 8, 1981.

McCullough, T.H. "Pat Carroll Pat Carroll Pat Carroll," *Drama-Logue*, January 13, 1983.

Martin, Marty. *Gertrude Stein Gertrude Stein Gertrude Stein*, New York: Vintage, 1980.

Young, Jordan R. Interview with Pat Carroll, July 13, 1988.

THE IRISH TRADITION

Dawson, Kevin. "Queen Billie," *Sunday Tribune*, Dublin, October 16, 1988.

Duffin, Shay. "Two Pints a Show — Behan's Aglow," *The Los Angeles Times*, December 3, 1978.

Edwards, Hilton. Introduction to Micheál Mac Liammóir, *The Importance of Being Oscar*, Dublin: Dolmen Press, 1963.

Goldstone, Patricia. "The Bloom of *Joyce's Women*," *The Los Angeles Times*, 1978.

Gussow, Mel. "The Quintessence of Beckett," *The New York Times*, November 20, 1970.

Hickey, Des and Smith, Gus. *A Paler Shade of Green*, London: Frewin, 1972.

Mitchell, Sean. "A portrait of the actress as six women," *The Los Angeles Herald Examiner*, November 3, 1985.

Rushe, Desmond. "Dublin: The Flourishing Trend of One-Man Shows," *The New York Times*, October 4, 1971.

Young, Jordan R. Interview with Eamon Morrissey, October 18, 1988.

EMILY, CHARLOTTE, ZELDA AND LILLIAN

Christon, Lawrence. "Julie Harris on the Fascinating Brontës," *The Los Angeles Times*, November 23, 1986.

Collins, William B. "Julie becomes a shy poetess," *Inquirer*, Philadelphia, October 10, 1976.

Drake, Sylvie. "Julie Harris — It's Ladies First," *The Los Angeles Times*, Sept. 5, 1985.

Dudar, Helen. "Shaping A Portait of A Playwright," *The New York Times,* January 12, 1986.

Harris, Julie, as told to Carragher, Bernard. "The *Belle* and the (Ex-)Buffoon," *Sunday Bulletin,* October 10, 1976.

_____. Interview. "Behind the Scenes of *The Belle of Amherst,*" promotional record issued by IBM in conjunction with TV broadcast, 1977.

Jack, Carolyn. "The last flapper," *The Palm Beach Post,* December 14, 1986.

Luce, William. *The Belle of Amherst,* Boston: Houghton Mifflin, 1976.

_____. Letter to the author, August 9, 1988.

Reilly, Charles Nelson. "From 60 characters to one," *Sun-Times,* Chicago, March 7, 1976.

HOMAGE TO BECKETT

Gussow, Mel. Interview with Jack MacGowran, January 9, 1973.

Unterecker, John and McGrory, Kathleen, eds. *Yeats, Joyce and Beckett,* Cranbury, N.J.: Associated University Press, 1976.

Young, Jordan R. *The Beckett Actor,* Beverly Hills, Ca: Moonstone Press, 1987.

_____. Interview with Barry McGovern, July 15, 1988.

_____. Interviews with Gloria MacGowran, June 22, 1975–June 5, 1979.

_____. Interview with Jack MacGowran, February 13, 1972.

_____. Interview with Donald McWhinnie, June 25, 1975.

MONOLOGUE: RAY STRICKLYN

Chandler, Charlotte and Stricklyn, Ray. *Confessions of a Nightingale,* New York: Samuel French, 1987.

Melville, Lee. "*Confessions* of Ray Stricklyn," *Drama-Logue,* March 19, 1987.

O'Steen, Kathleen. "Ray Stricklyn is Basking in *Nightingale* Limelight," *Variety,* March 11, 1987.

Young, Jordan R. Interview with Ray Stricklyn, August 4, 1988.

LIFE AS ART

Gray, Spalding. *Sex and Death to the Age of 14*, New York: Vintage, 1986.

_____. *Swimming to Cambodia*, New York: Theatre Communications Group, 1985.

Mitchell, Sean. "Swimming to Success," *The Los Angeles Herald Examiner*, April 5, 1987.

Young, Jordan R. Interview with Spalding Gray, April 26, 1989.

_____. Interview with Paul Linke, November 9, 1988.

_____. Interview with Shane McCabe, March 9, 1989.

_____. Interview with Mark Travis, March 11, 1989.

Additional information was gleaned from the pages of *American Theatre, American Theatre Annual, The Chicago Sun-Times, Current Biography, Drama-Logue, Hollywood Reporter, The Long Beach Press-Telegram, The Los Angeles Herald Examiner, Los Angeles Magazine, The Los Angeles Times, The New York Times, The New Yorker, The Orange County Register, The Oxford Companion to the Theatre, Theatre World, Variety* and *Who's Who in the Theatre.*

Index

Abe Lincoln in Illinois, 77
Ackerman, Bettye, 189-194
Act Without Words I, 148, 149
Acting Shakespeare, see *Ian McKellen Acting Shakespeare*
Actress, The, 38
Adrian, Max, 118, 119
Adventures of a Speculist, The, 15
Ages of Man, 23, 82, 83, 85, 87-89, 93, 195
Ages of Man, The, 85
Aleichem, Sholem, 29
All That Fall, 147, 149
Allen, Annulla, 55
Allen, Fred, 21
Allen, Woody, 178
Alsop, Scott, 32
Amadeus, 91
An Old Story, 38
Annulla, 55
Appearing Nitely, 48
As You Like It, 88, 93
Ashcroft, Peggy, 87
At Home, 17
At Wit's End, 61
Atkinson, Brooks, 42
Aubrey, John, 23, 64-65, 66
Autobiography of Alice B. Toklas, The, 102
Ballagh, Robert, 159
Banjo Dancing, 27-28
Bannister, Jack, 19
Bannister's Budget, 19
Barr, Richard, 43
Barrie, Frank, 19

Beach, Sylvia, 126
Beaches, 178
Beckett, Samuel, 25, 115, 121-124, 147-159
Beginning to End, 145, 151-155, 156, 159, 195, see also *End of Day*
Behan, Brendan, 115, 119, 121
Bein' with Behan, 121
Belle of Amherst, The, 6, 24, 60, 129-136, 141, 143, 190, 195
Belles of St. Trinians, The, 46
Bellin, Olga, 138
Ben Casey, 189
Bernard Shaw Story, The, 118-119
Bernhardt, Sarah, 21
Bigelow, Paul, 165
Billington, Michael, 89
Bingo, 89
Blasts and Bravos, 53, 54
Bogosian, Eric, 25
Bowden, Charles, 42-43
Boyden, Peter, 53
Brame, Charles, 33
Brando, Marlon, 81
Brendan, 121
Brief Lives, 64-65, 66, 196
Brighter Day, The, 74
Brontë, 24, 136-138, 143, 145, 196
Brontë, Charlotte, 136-138
Bronx Tale, A, 186
Brook, Peter, 152
Brother, The, 127
Bully, 55, 67
Burns, George, 69

Butler, Dean, 79
By George, 118, 119
Byron in Hell, 63
Caesar, Adolph, 25
Caesar's Hour, 101
Caldwell, Zoe, 53, 140, 144
Cale, David, 27
Candida, 45
Cappell, John, 79
Carey, George Saville, 14
Carradine, John, 52
Carroll, Pat, 22, 43, 99-113, 189, 191
Cat on a Hot Tin Roof, 161, 165
Chabert, Pierre, 122
Chandler, Charlotte, 167-168
CHiPs, 181
Churchill, 58, 62
Churchill, Winston, 22, 62
Cinque, Chris, 26
Clara's Heart, 178
Clarence Darrow, 55, 61,131
Climate of Eden, The, 161
Cocteau, Jean, 25
Coleridge, Samuel Taylor, 17
Colgan, Michael, 156
Collins, John, 16
Collins, Pauline, 19
Collins, William B., 133
Coming Into Passion/Song for a Sansei, 28
Company, 122, 123
Confessions of a Nightingale, 160-164, 166-171, 196
Confessions of an Irish Rebel, 121, 196
Corbin, John, 40
Corn is Green, The, 52
Countess, 138
Crisp, Quentin, 9, 173
Cummings, Constance, 19

Curchack, Fred, 24, 94, 95-97
Currer Bell, Esq., 136, see also Brontë
Dahr, Juni, 60
Dalí, Salvador, 161
Damon Runyon's Broadway, 53
Danny Thomas Show, The, 101
Darrow, Clarence, 64, 67
Dass, Baba Ram, 174
Dean, Philip Hayes, 31, 60
Death of a Salesman, 130
Devery, Mary Ellyn, 111, 112
Dewhurst, Colleen, 65
Diatribe of Love Against a Seated Man, 25
Dibdin, Charles, 16-17
Dickens, Charles, 40, 51-53
Dickinson, Emily, 5-6, 129-136, 141, 143
Dinner Cruise with Mark Twain, A, 79
Diversions of the Morning, The, 13-14
Divine Comedy, 26
Dodd, James Solas, 16
Donnelly, Donal, 119
Dotrice, Roy, 23, 58, 64-65, 66
Drake, Sylvie, 126, 183
Draper, Ruth, 5, 36-43, 45, 46, 47, 49, 52, 71, 106, 194
Drinking in America, 26
Dufau, Graciela, 25
Duffin, Shay, 115, 119-121, 127
Dukes, Gerry, 157
Dunaway, Faye, 140
Dylan Thomas Growing Up, 53
Edison, Thomas, 67
Edna His Wife, 43
Edwards, Hilton, 118
Einstein: The Man Behind the Genius, 62

Eleanor, 55, 67

Embers, 147, 149

Emlyn Williams as Charles Dickens, 51-53, 70, 84, 196

Encounter With an Interviewer, An, 69-70

End of Day, 148-149, 151, 152, see also *Beginning to End*

Endgame, 85, 122, 147, 148, 151, 156

Enough, 122

Enters, Angna, 27

Evening Brush, The, 16

Evening Lounge, 19

Evening with GBS, An, see *By George*

Evening with Mark Twain, An, 74, 79, 80

Evening with Quentin Crisp, An, 9, 173

Evening with — Who?, An, 99

Everybody's Autobiography, 102

Ezerbet Bathory: The Blood Countess, 33

Fantome de Marseille, Le, 25

Farber, Stephen, 91

Faulkner, William, 171

Feingold, Michael, 63

Ferrer, Jose, 155

Fielder, David, 159

Finnegan's Wake, 126

Fitzgerald, F. Scott, 138

Fitzgerald, Zelda, 138-139, 142, 143

Flanagan, Fionnula, 24, 124-127

Flanner, Janet, 53

Fletcher, Bramwell, 118-119

Fo, Dario, 27

Fonda, Henry, 55, 56, 61, 131, 169

Fonda, Jane, 140

Fool Show, The, 27

Foote, Samuel, 13-14, 17, 56

Footfalls, 122

Freed, Donald, 55, 58, 61-62, 138

Freeman, Stan, 61

Freud, Sigmund, 67, 186

From an Abandoned Work, 149

Frost, Ian, 63

Gallu, Samuel, 62

García Márquez, Gabriel, 25

Garland, Patrick, 65

Garrick, David, 13, 14, 21

Garry Moore Show, The, 47

Garson, Greer, 165

Gelb, Barbara, 65

Gelman, Larry, 62

Gertrude Stein Gertrude Stein Gertrude Stein, 98-113, 190, 191, 197

Gielgud, John, 23, 42, 82, 83-89, 90, 93, 94

Gillette, William, 21

Ginsberg, Allen, 174

Ginsberg, Eugenia, 24

Give 'Em Hell, Harry, 55, 59, 62, 63

Glass Menagerie, The, 167, 168

Goldberg, Whoopi, 5, 28

Goldman, William, 77, 119

Gontarski, S.E., 122

Gould, Harold, 67

Gray, Spalding, 26, 172, 173-179, 181, 183, 186

Gregory, Don, 131, 132

Grenfell, Joyce, 37, 44, 45-47, 49

Growing Up Queer in America, 26

Guidry, Frederick, 93

Guillory, Bennet, 30-31

Gussow, Mel, 122, 123

Hailey, Elizabeth Forsythe, 31

Hall, Philip Baker, 55, 58, 59

Hamlet, 21, 84, 85

Hannah Senesh, 29-30

Hansberry, Lorraine, 53
Happy Days, 123
Harris, Julie, 5-6, 24, 58, 110-111, 129-138, 145, 171, 186
Heckart, Eileen, 55
Heifetz, Jascha, 35
Helgeson, Timothy, 130, 132
Hellman, Lillian, 53, 139-141, 144
Henry IV, Part 2, 90
Here Are Ladies, 123-124, 126, 197
Herford, Beatrice, 40, 43
Hingle, Pat, 67
Hobson, Harold, 85
Hoiby, Lee, 49
Holbrook, Hal, 24, 53, 60-61, 67, 68-79, 81, 111, 187
Holbrook, Ruby, 69, 70
Holm, Celeste, 53
Home, 89
Hoover, Herbert, 62
Hoyle, Geoff, 27
Huckleberry Finn, 81
Hull, Henry, 74, 76, 79
Hunt, Linda, 55
Hunt, Peter, 63
I Am a Camera, 134
I Am a Woman, 28-29
I Must Be Talking to My Friends, 117
I'll Go On, 156-159, 197
Ian McKellen Acting Shakespeare, 83, 90-94, 155, 197
Iceman Cometh, The, 148
Importance of Being Earnest, The, 89
Importance of Being Oscar, The, 24, 116, 117-118, 197
Impossible Vacations, 178
In a Railway Station on the Western Plains, 42
Italian Lesson, The, 49

Jack MacGowran in the Works of Samuel Beckett, 155, see also *Beginning to End*
James Joyce's Women, 24, 124-127, 198
Jane Eyre, 136
Jenkins, Bunker, 75
Joan of Arc: Vision Through Fire, 60
Joffe, Roland, 175
Jones, James Earl, 60
Journey Into the Whirlwind, 24
Joyce Grenfell Requests the Pleasure, 46-47
Joyce, James, 124, 126
Joycemen, 127
Julia, 140
Julius Caesar, 86
Kahan, Gerald, 16
Katselas, Milton, 162
Kaufman, George, 21
Kavanaugh, Michael, 121
Kean, Edmund, 19
Kean, Moses, 19
Kemble, Fanny, 19
Kenny, Sean, 124
Kerouac, Jack, 174
Kerr, Walter, 133
Killing Fields, The, 175, 178
Kimmel, Joel, 61
Kingsley, Ben, 19
Knots Landing, 138
Krapp's Last Tape, 25, 147, 149
Kroll, Jack, 133
Krutch, Joseph Wood, 21
Lady's Name, A, 38
Lark, The, 134
Last Days of Patton, The, 139
Last Flapper, The, 139, 142, 143, 198, see also *Zelda*
Last of Mrs. Lincoln, The, 134

Laughton, Charles, 25, 52
Laurie, Piper, 138-139, 142, 143
Leachman, Cloris, 67
LeCompte, Elizabeth, 174, 175
Lecture on Mimicry, 14
Lecture on Tails, A, 16
Lecture upon Heads, 14-16
Lecture upon No-heads, A, 16
Lee, Garrett, 81
Lee, Peggy, 170
Leider, Jerry, 87
Leonard, Eric, 162
Letters of Edna St. Vincent Millay, The, 189
Levant, Oscar, 61
Lillian, 53, 139-141, 143-145, 198
Lincoln, Abraham, 64, 76
Lindfors, Viveca, 28-29
Linke, Francesca, 179, 182
Linke, Paul, 179-183, 184, 187
Lipman, Maureen, 49
Little Revue, The, 46
Living Lincoln, The, 33
Living on the Edge of Chaos, 28
Long Day's Journey Into Night, 78
Look Homeward, Angel, 174
Loos, Anita, 108
Lotas, John, 75
Love to All, Lorraine, 53
Love, William, 19
Lowell, Robert, 174
Luce Women, 145
Luce, William, 53, 129-133, 135-145, 190
Lumet, Baruch, 24
Lumet's Legends, 24
Macbeth, 90
McCabe, Shane, 184-186, 187
McCowen, Alec, 25, 33-35
McGovern, Barry, 147, 156-159

MacGowran, Gloria, 148, 156, 159
MacGowran, Jack, 122, 146-155, 156, 157, 159
McKellen, Ian, 83-84, 89-94, 95
McKenna, Siobhán, 123-124, 126
Macklin, Charles, 83
Mac Liammóir, Micheál, 24, 114, 116, 117-118
McLinn, Bill, 80, 81
Macready, William Charles, 19
McWhinnie, Donald, 149
Mad King Ludwig of Bavaria, 33
Magee, Patrick, 25
Mail Coach Adventure, The, 17
Malone Dies, 156, 157
Mandell, Alan, 122
Mann, Delbert, 136
Marceau, Marcel, 28
Mark Twain Himself, 80, 81
Mark Twain on Stage, 79
Mark Twain Tonight!, 24, 60, 68, 71-79, 198
Marowitz, Charles, 24
Martello, John, 53
Martin, Marty, 100, 103, 105, 109, 190
Mathews, Charles, 17-19
Medea, 140
Medina, Julio, 61
Member of the Wedding, The, 134
Mencken, H.L., 53, 54
Meredith, Burgess, 126
Merrick, Mike, 131, 132
Merry Wives and Widows, 101
Midsummer Night's Dream, A, 84
Millay, Edna St. Vincent, 189-191
Miller, Henry, 174
Mr. Gulliver's Bag, 127
Mister Lincoln, 62, 64
Mistero buffo, 27

Mitgang, Herbert, 62, 64
Molloy, 148, 154, 155, 156, 157
Mooney's Kid Don't Cry, 167
Moorehead, Agnes, 132
Morning, Leia, 33
Morrissey, Eamon, 115, 127
Morrow, John
Moses, Grandma, 67
Moss, Milton, 106-107, 110
Murder Has Been Arranged, A, 51
Murray, Rupert, 159
My Astonishing Self, 119
My Dinner with Andre, 178
My Gene, 65
na Gopaleen, Myles, 127
Naked Civil Servant, The, 173
Narita, Jude, 28
Nathan, George Jean, 43
Neumann, Frederick, 123
Night Must Fall, 51
Nixon, Richard, 55, 58, 59
No Man's Land, 89
No Place Like Home, 183-186, 198
Norcia, Patrizia, 49
O Briain, Colm, 159
O'Casey, Sean, 147
O'Connor, Carroll, 22, 118
O'Connor, Ulick, 121
O'Neill, Eugene, 65
Olivier, Laurence, 85, 89
Orwell, George, 161
Our Town, 178
Overland Mail, 19
Palmer, John, 16
Palminteri, Chazz, 186, 187
Papp, Joseph, 155
Paris '90, 45
Paris Was Yesterday, 53
Parker, Dorothy, 55
Paul Robeson, 30-31, 60

Performance Group, 174
Persoff, Nehemiah, 29, 30
Peters, Robert, 33
Philips, Lee, 131
Piaf, Edith, 25
Pleasure of His Company, The, 45
Plunderers, The, 162
Polanski, Roman, 152
Pond, James, 71, 75
Portraits of the Living and Dead, 16
Post, Ted, 191-194
Pueblo, The, 78
Quintero, Jose, 162
Rains, Claude, 52
Randall, Michael, 79
Ratner, Ellen, 26
Re:Joyce, 49
Readings and Music, 17
Redthroats, The, 27
Rehearsal, The, 13
Reid, Alec, 149
Reilly, Charles Nelson, 5, 129-131,
  135-139, 143
Reinhardt, Ray, 79-81
Rich, Allan, 133
Richard II, 85
Rintels, David, 61
Robeson, Paul, 60
Robeson, Paul Jr., 60
Rockabye, 122
Rogers, Will, 55-56, 57, 64
Romeo and Juliet, 101
Roosevelt, Franklin D., 63
Roosevelt, Teddy, 55
Rowan & Martin's Laugh-In, 47
Rumstick Road, 175
Runyon, Damon, 53
Rush, Barbara, 31, 32
Rushe, Desmond, 117
Rylands, George, 85, 90

St. Joan, 124
St. Mark's Gospel, 25, 33-35
Sandburg's Lincoln, 78
Satyrical Lecture on Hearts, 16
Saville, Jonathan, 93
Schechner, Richard, 174
Schechter, David, 29
School for Scandal, The, 89
Schull, Rebecca, 24
Scott, George C., 67, 139
Scott, Miss, 19
Scoundrel Time, 141
Search for Signs of Intelligent Life in the Universe, The, 26,48-49, 199
Secret Honor, 55, 58, 59,138, 199
Senator, The, 78
Senesh, Hannah, 29
Sex and Death to the Age of 14, 175
Shadow of a Gunman, The, 148
Shaffer, Peter, 91
Shakespeare, William, 23, 83-97
Shanks, Ann, 139
Shanks, Bob, 139
Shaw, George Bernard, 118-119, 121
Shaw, Harriet Weaver, 127
Shirley Valentine, 19
Sholem Aleichem, 29, 30
Shyre, Paul, 53, 54
Simms, Willard, 62
Skinner, Cornelia Otis, 37, 43-45, 71, 106, 132
Skinner, Otis, 43
Smart Aleck, 53, 63
Smith, Albert, 19
Sondergaard, Gale, 24
Spota, George, 56, 67, 74
Square Root of Soul, The, 25
Stackpole, John, 178
Stapleton, Jean, 49

Stapleton, Maureen, 140
Stein, Gertrude, 22, 99, 100, 102-110, 113
Stein, Leo, 109
Stevens, George Alexander, 14-16, 17
Stewart, Benjamin, 94-95
Stickney, Dorothy, 190
Stone, Arnold, 58
Streetcar Named Desire, A, 79, 161, 169
Streisand, Barbra, 140
Stricklyn, Ray, 160-171
Stronger, The, 38
Studdiford, Bill, 63
Stuff as Dreams Are Made On, 96-97, 199
Sullivan, Dan, 63-64
Sullivan, Ed, 74
Swift, Jonathan, 127
Swimming to Cambodia, 26, 172, 175-178, 179, 199
Talking About Yeats, 117
Tea With Lady Bracknell, 24
Teichmann, Howard, 63
Tempest, Marie, 38
Tempest, The, 93, 97
Terry, Ellen, 84, 87
Terry, Kate, 84
Terry, Marion, 84
Three Breakfasts, 41
Three Places in Rhode Island, 174-175, 178
Three Women and Mr. Clifford, 41
Thurber, 99
Thurber, James, 67
Time Flies When You're Alive, 179-183, 184, 187, 199
Toibin, Niall, 121
Tolstoy, Sonia, 138

Tom Sawyer, 81
Tomlin, Lily, 5, 25, 37, 47-49
Travis, Mark W., 179, 181, 182, 183-188
Truman, Harry S., 55, 59, 62-63, 64
Twain, Mark, 53, 60-61, 69-81, 178, 187
Tynan, Kenneth, 42, 89
Ultimate Seduction, The, 167
Ulysses, 124, 126, 127
Ulysses in Nighttown, 126
Unnamable, The, 156, 157
Vallee, Rudy, 9
Van Dyke, Elizabeth, 53
Ventriloquial Entertainment, 19
Venus and Adonis, 94, 200
Viertel, Jack, 62
Vieux Carré, 162, 167
Villa, 61-62
Villa, Pancho, 55
Voysey, Michael, 119
Wade, Stephen, 27-28
Wagner, Jane, 48, 49
Waiting for Godot, 122, 147, 148, 151, 156
Wayne, John, 164
Welles, Orson, 116
Wendkos, Gina, 26
Whitehead, Robert, 140
Whitelaw, Billie, 122

Whitmore, James, 24, 53, 55-56, 57, 58, 59, 62-63
Wilde, Oscar, 24, 117, 118
Wilkinson, Tate, 14, 17
Will Rogers' U.S.A., 24, 53, 55-56, 57, 67, 200
Williams, Dakin, 163-164
Williams, Emlyn, 51-53, 67, 84, 87
Williams, Tennessee, 161-169
Wilner, Lori, 29-30
Wilson, Edwin, 134
Windom, William, 67, 99
Wives of Henry VIII, The, 43
Wolfe, Kedric Robin, 26-27
Wolfe, Thomas, 174
Woman of Independent Means, A, 31-32, 200
Woman, 25
Wood, Audrey, 165
Woodward, Harry, 14
Woollcott, Alexander, 53, 63
Wooster Group, 174, 177
Worstward Ho, 123
Worth, Irene, 94, 95
Wright, Edward, 69, 70, 71
Yeats, William Butler, 124
Yorke, Lane, 138
Zabel, Morton D., 40, 41
Zelda, 138, see also *Last Flapper, The*

Also Available from Moonstone Press

THE BECKETT ACTOR
by Jordan R. Young • Foreword by Martin Esslin
This biography of Samuel Beckett's foremost interpreter reveals how Jack MacGowran changed forever the public perception of Beckett, from a purveyor of gloom and despair, to a writer of wit, humanity and courage. "A sparkling biography of a haunting and haunted man." — *Publishers Weekly*

LAUREL AND HARDY: THE MAGIC BEHIND THE MOVIES
by Randy Skretvedt • Foreword by Steve Allen
This behind-the-scenes documentary on the beloved comedy team tells how they made their classic comedies, and what happened during the making of them. Exclusive interviews and rare photographs. "Not only the best book on Laurel and Hardy ever assembled but also one of the best books on film comedy and Hollywood..." — *Kirkus Reviews*

SPIKE JONES AND HIS CITY SLICKERS
By Jordan R. Young • Foreword by Dr. Demento
The unauthorized biography of the legendary bandleader-comedian, who parlayed his cowbell-hiccup-and-gunshot renditions of popular songs into fame and fortune. "A treasurable piece of nostalgia... Record collectors will apreciate the lengthy discography." — *Booklist*

REEL CHARACTERS: GREAT MOVIE CHARACTER ACTORS
by Jordan R. Young • Foreword by Fritz Feld
Home video and cable TV have brought these unforgettable faces from Hollywood's Golden Era into millions of homes: twelve of Hollywood's best loved supporting players. "Photographs are copiously spread throughout the text, and the filmography for each actor is very detailed, including unbilled bits..." — *Library Journal*

LET ME ENTERTAIN YOU
by Jordan R. Young • Foreword by Leonard Maltin
Candid interviews with some of the top names in the entertainment world — discussing their careers, their successes and failures, their talents and shortcomings — are the focus of this fascinating book. "Glimpses of performers with their guards — and egos — lowered... younger readers will learn, older ones will reminisce and enthusiasts will enjoy." — *Publishers Weekly*

Ordering Information on Reverse

Order Form

Please send the following books:

Qty   Amount

____ *Acting Solo* paperback @ $11.95   _____
____ *Acting Solo* limited hardcover @ $21.95   _____
____ *The Beckett Actor* limited hardcover @ $24.95   _____
____ *Laurel and Hardy* paperback @ $14.95   _____
____ *Laurel and Hardy* limited hardcover @ $24.95   _____
____ *Spike Jones* paperback @ $14.95   _____
____ *Spike Jones* limited hardcover @ $19.95   _____
____ *Reel Characters* paperback @ $9.95   _____
____ *Reel Characters* limited hardcover @ $19.95   _____
____ *Let Me Entertain You* paperback @ $9.95   _____

Total for books   _____
Postage: add $1.75 for first book, .50 each additional   _____
California residents please add 6% tax   _____
Amount enclosed (U.S. funds)   _____

Ship to:

_____

_____

_____

IF THIS IS A LIBRARY BOOK, PLEASE PHOTOCOPY THIS PAGE.
ALL OUR BOOKS ARE PRINTED ON ACID-FREE PAPER.
SATISFACTION GUARANTEED OR PURCHASE PRICE REFUNDED.

MOONSTONE PRESS • P.O. Box 142 • Beverly Hills CA 90213